STONEY THE ROAD WE'VE TROD

MARTIN LUTHER JOHNSON

Stoney The Road We've Trod
Copyright © 2022 by Martin Luther Johnson.

This book is a work of now-fiction. Names of people and places have been changed to protect their privacy

No part of this book may be reproduced, stored in a retrieval system, or transmitted by any means, electronic, mechanical, photocopying, recording, or otherwise, without written permission from the author.

ISBN: 978-1-952302-93-0 (sc)
ISBN: 978-1-957009-50-6 (hc)
ISBN: 978-1-957009-52-0 (e)

Library of Congress Control Number: 2022905428

CONTENTS

PREFACE v

ACKNOWLEDGEMENTS 1

CHAPTER I INTRODUCTION 3

CHAPTER II CHATTEL SLAVERY IN THE UNITED
    STATES 9

CHAPTER III THE SLAVE'S SURVIVAL OF SLAVERY 40

CHAPTER IV THE FREEDOM MOVEMENTS 68

CHAPTER V NATHANIEL PAUL'S STRUGGLES FOR
    THE ABOLITION OF SLAVERY 92

CHAPTER VI DAVID WALKER'S CONCEPT OF
    FREEDOM 107

CHAPTER VII AN ANALYSIS OF DAVID WALKER'S
    APPEAL 145

CHAPTER VIII CONCLUSION 180

BIBLIOGRAPHY 189

ABOUT THE AUTHOR 197

PREFACE

Liberation, Abolition and Freedom are words that have the potential, on the one hand, to incite anger, hostility, war, and even open rebellion, while on the other hand, there is the possibility and hope that other emotion that is more cordial and productive in they struggle to achieve the ends which liberation, abolition, and freedom seek to accomplish. Liberation, abolition, and freedom are perhaps some of the most misunderstood words used within the context of human societies. They are relative words that take on meaning and significance depending on the society in which they are used. The societies and the relevant cultures tend to define the words and their applicability based upon the perceived intent of the persons, or organizations that used them as a part of their technical nomenclature. But whether used or implied, the words are as old as humanity. For there are no peoples on planet earth that have not, at some time, used the words, behaved in such manner as to desire the end product of them, or have led open revolts and rebellions to achieve the benefits of those ideals both implied and inherent within those words.

The initial criticism from those for whom freedom is a given is that of dismay, anger, and even rejection. While others will dismiss the idea by raising the question: Why another book on Liberation, Abolition, and Freedom? Each of which is a valid and relevant question. But why another book on liberation, abolition, and freedom is not the foremost question, the piercing question is: Why not? Why not engage in further pursuits to better understand what has been and is the plight of Afro-Americans in the "Home of the brave and the Land of the 'free'?' Perhaps the initial response to producing another work on David Walker will come in the form of another question, "Did David Walker produce enough works to comprise a whole book*" Scholarship is both concerned about what a person did, what a person said and what is implied in a person's behavior and character.

In this work, an effort is made to delve beneath the overt betray or of David Walker and to ascertain significance and meaning from those aspects of Walker's life and behavior that might have escaped the eyes of previous visitors to his works. Because scholarship and research are more tentative than conclusive, it becomes the task of each visitor to the data to not only visit and consider what others have said about the subject, but also to find additional implications and significance that might have escaped previous visitors, and say and report what they have failed to find and report.

I am convinced that the core of both Old and New Testaments has to do with liberation, abolition, and freedom. However, these concepts and ideals are not simply processes and procedural steps taken toward liberation, abolition, and freedom, rather they are actual states of being that are seen, felt, and are experienced by enslaved, dehumanized, minimized, and disenfranchised humans the world over. Therefore, to talk about liberation implies abolitionist efforts with the results being freedom. But abolition that leads to freedom is not simply liberation, it also involves freedom to become. This runs counter to emancipation from American slavery and then the return to slavery by instituting slaves' codes and Jim Crows Laws which tend to re-enslave those persons recently freed. The message of the Judeo-Christian Bible, in essence, suggests that after liberation from slavery, there must be a Promised Land of freedom in Canaan. Therefore, deliverance implies the ushering in of freedom. This is essentially portrayed in the Exodus event and is further articulated in the Lukan narrative (Luke 4: 18- 20). There can be no New Testament sermon preached that has any relevancy to the message of Jesus Christ unless there is included within, liberation, abolition, and freedom. The Christian practice must be consistent with the Holy Bible in all aspects of human relationships. The Christian message does not set a standard of relationships that are applicable to China and Africa, that are to operate in the Protestant pulpits of America between eleven and twelve O'clock on Sunday morning and are discarded the remainder of the week. The Christian message of liberation does not suggest that you love and respect as equal every Chinese in China or every African in Africa as long as they all remain in China and in Africa. There must be a consistency between the teaching of the Holy Bible and the Christian practice. The message of the Christian bible transcends all humanly manufactured boundaries that separate and render one human inferior to another human. If one misuses this aspect of the message of the historical Jesus, then one has missed the centrality of Christian theology. There can be no genuine, authentic, relevant Christianity without liberation. However, liberation and freedom are not limited to, nor totally determined by humans and social institutions and societies, the foundation stone upon which liberation and freedom rest are the God of nature and nature's God. Therefore, liberation and freedom are not qualities nor states of being bequeathed to humans by political Sovereign powers. Those persons and institutions involved in the Liberation struggle, "Hold these truths to be self-evident that all men are created equal..."

While "Black Power" is a relatively recent term used in the vocabulary of African America Black Power advocates, abolition, racial liberation arid slave freedom are words and concepts that are as old as America, and slavery itself. These concepts are very much a part of the Bill of Rights, the Declaration of Independence, and the Constitution of the United States of America. But while America — the thirteen original colonies — was flexing muscles to become free of its Mother Country, the chattel slave — although not well organized — was flexing his muscles to become free of those social, racial, economic, and political bonds designed to render him and his posterity slaves for life. It was from the great and creative mind of Frederick Douglas that came these:

"If there is no struggle, there is no progress. Those who Profess to favor freedom, and yet depreciate agitation, are men who want crops without plowing up the ground. They want rain without thunder and lightning ...This Struggle may be a moral one: or it may be a physical one, or it may be both moral and physical; but there must be a Struggle."

These words essentially express the words of Henry Highland Garnet "Let your Motto be Freedom."

The concept of freedom is not a new phenomenon to human beings in general or to the Black man in particular. The aspiration for freedom has been a part of the human psyche since time immemorial. However, in each society known to man, there have always been some forms of social concerns that have catapulted certain individuals into the limelight and forefront of history and social involvement social problems have manifested themselves in varieties of forms and have revealed themselves in different forums from culture to culture. The attempt to eradicate from societies these kinds of problems has led men onto battlefields that have involved the nations' military might — as was experienced during the Civil War in the United States of America —, in street demonstrations, legislative decisions, and even in pamphlets, such as David Walker's Appeal of 1829. Because Black Americans are the only ethnic minority in the United States of America upon whom discrimination and social injustices have been perpetrated solely on the basis of color, the Black Liberation Struggle has taken on a uniquely differently form, approach, and goal that have differed from the approaches used by other ethnic groups. The badge of color by which blacks are identified demanded a new plan and strategy. Historically, America has been obsessed with color has been a badge of differentiation and separation, a sign of and a basis for racial inferiority and superiority that has created in the mind of a significant segment of the white community a ground for subjugation to slavery. Perhaps this was a pervading motivation for Henry Highland Garnet's positive stance that led to his vociferous expression and admonition: "Let your motto be resistance! Resistance! Resistance! Historically, no persons have ever won their freedom without resorting to some forms of overt resistance to the system, or to the persons who held them in bondage. This book has as its perspective a Constructive effort to explain the plight of David Walker and his struggle for the total freedom of the slaves in America. While Walker predates Frederick Douglas, Denmark Vesey, Martin Luther King, Jr., and a large number of relatively modern social reformers. None, he ends as a beacon light of hope for his generation, and his works have provided sources of strength for generations to come as the struggle for freedom continues. There are a number of theologians who seek to do theology from the white perspective, and some of their works reject a genuine authentic effort to be true to the task: however, it is a totally different challenge to do theology that is relevant when one does not emerge from, nor represent the culture one seeks to address. Their theology is, at best, an approximation. Therefore, in order that the true pains and sufferings of oppressed people to be fully addressed, it is extremely important that the black community continues to produce credible theologians who are a part of the faith they seek to express and represent the community they seek to address.

STONEY THE ROAD WE'VE TROD:
David Walker's Concept of Freedom

Martin Luther Johnson

ACKNOWLEDGEMENTS

I am grateful to the Staff Librarians at New York University for their in- valuable assistance during my four-year tenure there as a student. To the librarians at Baylor University, The University of Central Texas, Princeton University, and Monmouth University, Long Branch, New Jersey for the many hours of professional assistance during the research stages of the work.

My sincerest appreciation also to Professor Robert C. Briggs, who "shocked me out of my dogmatic slumber"', to Professor Norma Thompson at New York University, a caring and kind Religious Educator who inspired me to study; to Mr. C. Spencer Pompey, who is now resting with his God, and Mrs. Hattie Ruth Pompey, who were towers of strength and sources of inspiration for me during my academic pilgrimage; to my mother, Mrs. Aldoro Johnson, who now sleeps with The Lord, who through her persistent discipline, provided loving concern for me during the course of my earliest development: to my family, much of whose time I used during the extended periods of study, thanks!

To the hundreds of friends and colleagues, many of whom now have their names listed in the Lamb's Book of life, Thanks! To the Mount Olive Holy Temple Church family, the most patient and caring people in the world, upon whom I practiced a variety of homiletical skills and theological understandings, Thanks! Hopefully, the Lord will reward them for their endurance. Lastly, to icy typists for their many hours of dedication and precision during the typing of the final drafts of the book and getting it ready for publication, to Professor Harvey C. Pittman for his pastoral skills and professional guidance as I progressed through the process of this work that led to the presentation and successful defense of the work, Thanks!

CHAPTER I

INTRODUCTION

This book addresses the concept of freedom in the works of David Walker, who lived during 1785-1830. The book also provides insights that help determine the relevance of Walker's concept of freedom for the liberation struggle of the Black Church in the United States during the period 1830-1865. This book specifically demonstrates David Walker's social, political, and economic efforts to rid the Nation of slavery. Secondly, the book focuses on the involvement of black leaders in the Black Churches, and the abolitionist movements as they sought to end Chattel slaves in the United States of America.

The freedom struggle in the United States, historically, is one of the boldest efforts ever undertaken by the Black community to rid the Nation of slavery. The efforts involved committed persons in a freedom struggle that occupies an extensive period of American history in general and, a long period of Black history specifically. The concepts of freedom that were espoused by David Walker, as well as those concepts espoused by his predecessors, Nathaniel Paul and Richard Allen are examined for their effect on walker's development. Both Paul's and Allen's lives overlapped the period 1755-1785, the period immediately before the birth of Walker in 1785. Both Paul and Allele were closely connected to religious movements and were strong advocates of the freedom of man.

David Walker was born a free man in Wilmington, North Carolina, in 1785, a city in which he had seen the horrors of the slave systems first-handed as they were seen and experienced by black people. He moved away from Wilmington, North Carolina at an early age and settled in Boston, Massachusetts. From Boston, he commenced efforts that had the ultimate aim of freedom for the slaves. Walker's antislavery attitude was born out of his experiences of disdain for the slave system. Walker was also moved by his existential situation and by the slave status quo of his time. Walker found it quite inconsistent that the words of the Declaration of Independence were not a reality for the slave, thus he frequented forums where the opportunity was available to articulate anti-slavery sentiments. Freedom's Journal printed in the 1830s, recorded several occasions on which Walker was accorded such opportunity.

By the time of Walker's birth in 1785, the "Invisible Institution" was already involved in the freedom struggle.' Thus Walker did not pioneer the freedom struggle in America, but joined in the struggle and added the power of his pen to the struggle. In addition to the efforts of Paul and Allen, the Reverends George Leile and Andrew Bryan had entered the freedom struggle by organizing the first Negro Baptist church in America in Savannah, Georgia in 1773. To break away from the confines of white religion and organize a religious group that was totally led and controlled by blacks was a direct protest against the slaveocracy of the south. An understanding of the works of these pioneers of"[1] the freedom struggle way helps to bring about radical changes in social attitudes and will enhance the individual appreciation of the struggle for freedoms in America.

Historically, black religion has been viewed as primarily otherworldly and somewhat detached from the existential situation of a suffering people whose lot was chattel slavery. However, religion for men like David Walker was not ...the sign of the oppressed creature, the heart of the heartless anti-world ... the spirit of the spiritless situation." Slave religion was not necessarily ... the opium of the people".[2] While black religion does tend to focus quite heavily upon the other-worldly and life after death, those foci have not substituted for, nor have they diverted the black man's attention front the struggles for freedom in this world.

This book investigates the dual role of the black man's religion as not only otherworldly but also this-worldly The concept of freedom as espoused by David Walker was not only based upon his reading of the Holy

---

[1] Franklin Frazier and Eric C. Lincoln. <u>The Negro in America and the Black Church Since Frazier</u>. (New York: Schocken Books, 1974), pp. 21-24.

[2] Karl Marx and Friedrich Engels. <u>On Religion</u>. (New York: Schocken Books, 1964). p.42.

Bible, was also based upon the words of the Declaration of Independence, the Constitution of the United States, and, the writings of Americans such as Henry Clay, and Patrick Henry, Thomas Jefferson. Walker sought to actualize the will of God in the lives of the slaves, as he understood it so that freedom would become a reality for them also.

David Walker joined the ranks of a large number of religious leaders and social reformers who were actively involved in efforts, movements, and organizations whose aim was the ultimate and eventually social and political liberation of the slaves. The evidence of such efforts is found in sermons, speeches, songs, and black religious and revolutionary events. Since a number of theologians, sociologists, anthropologists, and historians have alluded to the possible significance of black religion's involvement in, and the impact it might have had upon the freedom struggle, there is an opportunity to add new insights to current scholarship as to the role of a specific black leader based upon his concept of freedom.

The concept of freedom has been a part of human aspiration since time immemorial. However, in each society known to man, there have always been social problems that have catapulted certain individuals into the forefront of social involvement. Social problems have manifested themselves in a variety of forms and in different situations from culture to culture. The attempts and efforts to eradicate these problems have led men onto battlefields that involved the Nation's military might (as was seen during the Civil War in the United States of America), street demonstrations, legislative decisions and, even pamphlets and appeals, such as David Walker's Appeal of 1829.

Freedom has been one of the battle cries of Americans since the Declaration of Independence and the formation of the democratic republic known as the United States of America. The cry for freedom has not been a unique cry of any one single ethnic or racial group, for at some juncture in each nation's history and in people's lives, there have been some feelings of discrimination and social injustice which led to cries for freedom. However, black Americans are the only ethnic minority in the United States against whom discrimination and social injustices have been perpetrated solely on the basis of color.

The concept of freedom as seen in Walker's works, and as an element of biblical religion has always held specific weaning for the slave and for black religion. While the primary function of this research is to focus on the concept of freedom in the works of David Walker, one cannot accurately understand and appreciate Walker apart from his religious orientation and his relationship to the Black church. Religion for Walker was not necessarily a dispassionate, erudite expression of his tradition, culture, and way' of" life: it was also a means of expressing verbally and non-verbally, the internal feelings, external experiences, and convictions that there do exist in the universe and in one's life, an infinite power to whom finite beings owe reverence and allegiance. For Walker religion was not simply a conviction, it was also a powerful force that motivated man to decisive, positive, and, possible revolutionary actions.[3]

This study isolates the aspect and concept of freedom in Walker's speeches and writings and surfaces what was the driving force in his life that led to decisive actions. There are several reasons why a study of Walker's life as it reflects his struggle for freedom is important. One is because of the question raised by the researcher regarding the missing link between his life in North Carolina and the transition to Boston and, the persons influencing his behavior. Secondly, there is some question as to his actual writing of the Appeal; thirdly, neither historians nor theologians have done justice to his historical and theological contributions. David Walker has been dead physically for one hundred and sixty-five years, but the final chapter of his life and contributions is still open and awaits additional, tentative, conclusions.

---

[3] Donald M. Jacobs. "David Walker: Boston Race Leader, 1825-1830". (Essex Institute Historical Collections, 1971), pp. 94- 107.

CHAPTER II

CHATTEL SLAVERY IN THE UNITED STATES

The primary struggle of humanity is freedom! The forms and approaches that struggle has taken have fluctuated based upon the nature of each prevailing situation, and forces of history. However, the existence of slavery in the new world (the thirteen original Colonies) presents a new set of dynamics in the long history of slavery and subjugation that is known to man; slavery in America was predicated essentially upon race and skin pigmentation. Slavery in the United States is a dark chapter in the Nation's history, the ripple effects of which continue to be seen and felt in every aspect of the fiber of America.[4] What began as an effort to seek out new lands, explore unknown regions, and develop a democratic republic where freedom, justice, and equality were realized hallmarks, eventually degenerated to

---

[4] Henry Clay Bruce. The New Man: Twenty-Nine Years As A Slave, Twenty-Nine Years As A Freeman. (York, Pennsylvania: Anstadt Press, 1895), pp. 45-46.

one of the cruelest forms of man's inhumanity to a man known to civilized man. Slavery itself, historically, was not necessarily inherently cruel and inhumane; rather slavery was a significant milestone reached by an ancient man on his road to civilization.

Prior to slavery, those prisoners that were taken in wars were slaughtered; therefore, slavery was a slight transition from barbarism to civilization. The institution of slavery allowed the victor to spare the victim's life, instead, subjugating him to a period of servitude, not on the basis of color, but on the basis of a war victim. The aspect of slavery in the United States that catapults it into history as being unique is that an institution was allowed to exist based purely upon pigmentation of the skin and the superficial posting assumption of biological inferiority of blacks to whites.[5] Human slavery was not a new phenomenon unique to the black experience in Africa or in the New World. Slavery was practiced in Africa between various tribal groups who found themselves engaged in inter-tribal wars. During the inter-tribal wars, people were captured and subsequently subjected to slavery or servanthood where cruelty was an inevitable consequence. However, the concept of slavery predicated upon the perception of racial inferiority was not a part of the social and mental psyche among African slave-owners as was the reality in America.[6] Among the ancient Egyptian,

---

[5] Kenneth M. Stampp. The Peculiar Institution. (New York: Alfred A. Knopf. 1969), pp I 5- 17.

[6] Ibid., pp. 8-9.

Greek and Roman Empires, peoples of various national origins were enslaved, but menial servitude was not tantamount to degradation, nor synonymous with the inferiority of the captured persons. It was in the United States that occurred the harshest and most inhumane form of slavery known to mankind. Slavery in America was based upon the ostensible belief that the subject was biologically and mentally inferior to the master or slave master.[7]

Chattel slavery in the United States was an economic and political institution that was allowed to degenerate into a socio-racial system that robbed the subjects of their external status of equality and, was an attempt to rob them of the feelings of their inherent worth and dignity. Slavery was a testimony to the internal and external insensitivity of the Western mentality to the humanity and personhood of the slave during the nineteenth century. It is rather imperceptible to the present writer that the intellectual authentications of the slave system along with economic adventurers would be so naive as to believe, in light of European intellectual enlightenment, that the black person was biologically and mentally inferior to the white person. Their positions were based more upon cultural and ethnocentric perceptions than upon scientific validations.[8] Nevertheless, both the pro-slavery and anti-slavery arguments persisted throughout the slave era

---

[7] John Hope Franklin. From Slavery to Freedom. (New York: Allied A. Knopf. 1967). pp. 42-44.

[8] Ibid., pp. 8-9.

in the United States with each camp espousing, either hypocritically or honestly, their gut-level feelings and perceptions about slavery.

Chattel slavery and the horrors of the system is an eternal aspect of American history that shall always serve as a reminder of human capabilities when greed and the perception of cultural and biological superiority persist. In a real sense, America has essentially two histories, at least: the history of whites who came on the "Mayflower" and blacks who came on slave ships, called: "Morning Star", "Charity", "Young Saint Paul", and "Good Intent."

To keep before the American consciousness, the wide divergences between the two histories, there evolved the incessant protest movements whose ultimate objectives were to further point out the gross injustices and the appalling inconsistencies between democracy and chattel slavery and to rid America of a colossal social ill. Chattel slavery, as the system later developed in the original colonies, seems to have come about after 1619, when a Dutch cargo ship with twenty Africans aboard arrived at the port in Jamestown, Virginia. Little did anyone know that the arrival of this "species of property" would eventually degenerate into chattel slavery as opposed to indentured servitude.[9] The next two hundred years would reflect a new chapter in the history of man's relationship with a man. Historians, sociologists, and politicians have argued that slavery

---

[9] Stanley M Elkins. Slavery. (Chicago: The University of Chicago Press. l968). pp. 3-4. 206-207.

was an economic system necessary to the growth of the Nation in general and the growth of the South specifically. Kenneth M. Stampp is quite perceptive in his treatment of the development of the slave system in America: "The slave-plantation system answered no 'specific need' that could not have been answered in some other way... the rise of slavery in the South was inevitable only in the sense that every event in history seems inevitable after it has occurred."[10] Carl N. Degler, interestingly raises the specific question that gets at the core of the slave system in America. Degler's question is in the form of a thesis in his article. "Slavery and the Genesis of American Race Prejudice." Degler's provocative thesis is that slavery did not cause race prejudice, rather, it was race prejudice that caused slavery. Degler is suggesting that the slave master's feelings of superiority over the Africans led to the African's enslavement. It is perceived by the present writer that the cause of racial prejudice is not either/or, but rather, both and the same. The fact that there existed a slave system in America presents the inevitable possibility of affirming to succeeding generations of whites a perception of an unequaled inherent worth and inferiority of the slave to the slave master.[11] The slave's social status suggested that he was less than the master.

---

[10] Kenneth M. Stampp. The Peculiar Institution. (New York: Alfred A. Knopf, 1969). pp. 4-6.

[11] Carl N. Degler. Slavery and the Genesis of American Race Prejudice. Studies in History and Society II. (October 1959). pp. 49-66.

Therefore, the initial perception of the African by his white captors was that of inferiority and thus, prejudice.

Chattel slavery, race prejudice, and tire perceptions of the inferiority of blacks by whites are vividly seen in the treatment of blacks during the slave era. Herbert Aptheker advances a concise definition of slavery that not only defines the system but describes its horrors: "Slavery was systematized cruelty." The slaves became a non-entity, an object of abuse, a machine, and a means to an end rather than an end within themselves. Chattel slavery was the exploitation of one human being by another based upon prejudice, and feelings of superiority with the ultimate goal of realizing an economic profit from slave labor.[12] Color was, for the slave master, a badge of inferiority, a reason for suspicion, and a just cause to subjugate to slavery. Black became synonymous with evil, the devil, and something less than good and perfect. This negative connotation of blackness penetrates early American literature from poetry and short stories to political essays and religious sermons. The Jew can change continents, change his name, and be accepted as white. The European can change his accent, come to America, move into an exclusive community, and be eventually accepted as a white American. But the black person, regardless of his change of continent, accent, and community, is still black. Blackness becomes a badge of eternal identity.[13]

---

[12] Herbert Aptheker. Essays in the History of the American Negro. (New York: International Publishers. 1964), pp. 8-10.

[13] Thomas Jefferson. Notes on Virginia. (New York: Random House. 1944). p. 256.

Color is the initial aspect of the individual seen by another and, as it relates to blacks, immediately suggests a difference in the minds of white Americans. The color was also a concern of one of America's greatest thinkers, Thomas Jefferson. Jefferson wrote in his Notes in the State of Virginia in 1781 that "the first difference that strikes us is that of color." Jefferson further articulates his perception of the lower social category into which color assigns one by suggesting that "this unfortunate difference of color and perhaps of faculty is a powerful obstacle to the emancipation of these people."[14] While Benjamin Banneker, a noted black scientist, strongly opposed and refuted Jefferson's theory by accentuating his individual accomplishments as a black person, the Jeffersonian perception still prevailed, and it was not uniquely Jeffersonian during eighteenth-century America. Winthrop Jordan is quite perceptive in positing that Jefferson's perception is quite typical during the eighteenth century, and further testifies to the white man's fascination and the problem with color.[15] It was incumbent upon the slaveocracy to arrive at what seemed to be a logical social, political, economic, racial, and biblical rationale upon which the slave system was justifiable. With the color of the slave as a distinctive external physical phenomenon, the slave master had available to him another natural criterion upon which to advance the theory of black inferiority and, thus

---

[14] Ibid., p. 262.
[15] Silvo A. Bedini. The Life of Benjamin Banneker. (New York: Charles Scribner's Sons, 1972), p. 152.

a further justification of slavery. The drawing of the color line between master and slave was a deliberate obsession and a daily preoccupation of the master. Color became the chief external criterion in distinguishing between master and slave and the establishment of the perceived inherent worth of the black slave. To satisfy the superior ego and feelings of the slave master's greater self-worth, it was necessary for him to degrade his "species of property." This was accomplished by relegating him, the slave, to the edges of society and subjugating him to second-class status, postulating that he was a savage and, brute and that he was destined by God, the Creator, to remain a slave for life.[16]

Chattel slavery in the United States was born, harbored, nurtured, and allowed to thrive based upon racism: racism led one color of people to enslave another color of people. Slavery was not merely an effort to exploit a person; had that been the case, the Indian and the white European servants and their posterity would have been assigned to perpetual slavery. There was no form of agricultural labor for which blacks were more adequately suited than their counterparts. The theory and myth of blacks being worn suitable for developing farmland and agricultural labor was always an insidious and subtle attempt to justify slavery because even slavery, they seemed to say, had a good ultimate end. Frederick Law Olmsted, while traveling through the Deep South, noted that on many occasions whites were

---

[16] Leslie Howard Owens. The Species of Property, (New York: Oxford University Press, 1976), pp. 9-13

performing essentially the same tasks as blacks under identical conditions "at work in the hottest sunshine ... in the regular cultivation of cotton."[17]

To perpetuate the Negro's slave status, the theory was soon advanced that his color and "certain racial traits" rendered the Negro more suitable for bondage than his white masters, or the white servants. But with an extraordinary amount of visible data testifying to the contrary, it became increasingly incumbent upon Southerners to amass credible data to authenticate their positions on the suitability of the Negro for slavery by validating his inherent inferiority as less than a person. As the vocal racist arguments headed to self-destruct, Southerners resorted to a number of academic disciplines in an effort to justify slavery. Dr. Samuel W. Cartwright, of Louisiana, defended Negro inferiority by arguing that "the visible difference in skin pigmentation also extended to 'the membranes, the muscles, the tendons, and ... (to) all the fluids and secretions', even the Negro's brain and nerves, the chyle(sic) and all the honors are tinctured with a shade of the pervading darkness."[18] There were others who represented extreme views by saying that Negroes and whites did not belong to the same species. While one might disagree with that position from a biological perspective, there were those within the slave community who would totally agree that the nature of

---

[17] Debow's Review, XXI. (Southern Cultivator, II, 1858), pp. 22-23
[18] Fredrick Law Olmsted. A Journey in the Back Country, (New York 1860), pp. 298, 349-350

the slave master's treatment of his slaves suggests that whites and blacks derived from different origins. The cruel, atrocious, and inhumane capabilities of the slave masters are nowhere more graphically described than in the words of one, Adeline Cunningham, born as a slave in slavery days who said "the white folks were rough people and day treat everybody rough ...No such, we never goes to church. Times we sneak in de woods and prays de Lawd (sic) to make us free and times one of the slaves got happy and made a noise dat dey heard at the de big house and den de overseer come and whip us 'cause we prayed de Lawd to set us free."

Another ex-slave, Williams Grimes, cites the horrors of the slave system as he discussed the response he received from his master. Grimes had worked all night to complete a job that sickness the previous day had prevented him from doing. Grimes stated that the master made him work at night, and flogged him because he had not done enough:

"It seems as though I should not forget this flogging when I die; it grieved my soul beyond the power of time to cure. I should not have been alive now if I had remained a slave, for I would have resisted with my life when I became older, treatment which I have witnessed towards others, and ... such as I have received when a boy from overseers."[19]

The scholarship is not unanimous on the severity of the slave system. For there are scholars who advance

---

[19] James B. Sellers. Slavery in Alabama. (Tuscaloosa Alabama: University of Alabama Press, 1950), pp. 344-345.

the proposition that slavery was a humane and humanitarian system designed to elevate the condition of the slave. That proposition suggests that slavery was a school whose curriculum was ultimately beneficial to the slave. The essence of the basic argument was that slavery and the plantation system were the best schools to facilitate the orderly transition of the Africans from their barbaric lifestyles to the civilized culture of the white wan. However, there were, at least, associated with those presuppositions one fallacy and one contradiction: one was that the Africans were totally void of civilization, and, secondly, the slaves were given no diplomas, nor did they have a graduation day from the slave system.

Chattel slavery in the United States of America was also given credence based upon the assertion that the African possessed a beastly nature, that he was a savage. and had no religious beliefs. Winthrop D. Jordan is of the same position that is quoted in Charles H. Nichols during the initial European contact with the Africans, there immediately appeared certain physical, social, and behavioral anomalies that determined for them certain criteria that made the African a most likely candidate for slavery.[20] The native African was different from the European white man in color, culture, religion, and in external physical appearance. Jordan further accentuated that, unfortunately, the slave trader whose

---

[20] Nichols, Charles H. Many Thousand Gone: The Slaves and their Freedom. (Don Mills, Ontario: Fitzhenry & Whiteside, Limited, 1969), pp. 38-40.

primary motives were influenced by their adventurous spirit and wrote the first descriptions of West Africa. He further perceived that there was very little interest in the conversion of the native Africans, initially, rather, there was an interest in economic exploitation and the expansion of English society into the New World.[21]

While the above-mentioned observations are Jordan's, there were such reputable scholars as E. Franklin Frazier. John Hope Franklin, Lerone Bennett, and Gunnar Myrdal, to cite a few, seem to utilize Jordan's premise as a point of departure to arrive at a basic understanding of the initial encounter between the African and the Europeans. The slave trader's assumption of a beastly behavior, a savage nature, and non-Christian religious practices of the slave were all aspects of the African that differed from that of the European and, was, therefore, a legitimate basis upon which the white man could stand to judge the slave as being less civilized than the European counterparts.[22] The initial encounter between the Englishman and the African presented a new challenge on the one hand, and on the other hand, a new possibility for the Englishman. On the one hand, he was challenged to formulate a position of relationship with the African while on the other hand he saw within the color differentiation the possibility for exploitation. To posit

---

[21] Winthrop D. Jordan. White Over Black: American Attitudes Towards the North: 1150-1812. (Chapel Hill, North Carolina: University of North Carolina Press, 1972). pp. 3-4.

[22] Winthrop D. Jordan. The Whiteman's Burden (New York: Oxford University Press, 1974), pp, 3-4

that the Englishman's encounter with the African was the first time that they had seen people of color is a gross error; there had been contacted between people of color for generations. As early as the sixteenth century, travelers had begun to comment on various sightings of people with black skin. On a voyage made to the coast of Guinea and to the Indies of Nova Hispania, in 1564, M. John Hawkins cites an interesting aspect of the culture of the natives, "these people are all blacks, and are called Negroes, without any apparel, saving before their privities." Further attestation of the obvious difference between the European and the native African is prolifically stated in Robert Baker's narrative poem reflective of his observations during two voyages to the West African coast in 1562 and 1563. He described the native African in the following manner:

> And entering in (a river), we see a number of blacks soules, Whose likeliness seem'd men to be, but all as blacks as coles. Their Captains comes to me as naked as my naile, Not having witte or honestie to cover once his tail.[23]

An obvious prejudice is expressed in lines two and three of the above quote, Whose likeliness seem'd men to be, but all as blacks as coles ... which inherently suggest, by the conjunction "but", that their blackness was the discriminator between being men and savage beasts.

---

[23] Winthrop D. Jordan. <u>White Over Black: American Attitudes Toward the North</u> (Chapel Hill, North Carolina: The University of North Carolina Press,1972), pp, 3-4.

These fallacies emerged out of a deliberate misunderstanding of the African cultural history and background. The word primitive, for the slave traders, meant outdated, outmoded, and irrelevant. Kenneth M. Stampp is indeed positive in his treatment of the level of "civilized" accomplishment the Africans had reached. Prior to the advent of the English and American slave trade, the native Africans already developed an agricultural economy that reflected as "complex" and "organization of a plantation system." The Yorubas and Binis of Nigeria, the Mandingos and Hausas of western Sudan, the people of Dahomey, and a number of the tribes of the Congo were people of settled agriculture who engaged in trade and commerce with the outside world.[24] Therefore, to portray these people as beasts, savages who led animal-like lives is a vast distortion of truth and is a further attempt to justify the slavery in America, with all of the horrors the system represented.[25]

The black image in the wind of the white man has contributed to chattel slavery in the United States of America. For the white man, (the slave traders and early travelers to West Africa), the color black was obviously different, and the difference was tantamount to being less than the mainstream culture as espoused by the Europeans. The nineteenth-century white

---

[24] The First Voyage of Robert Baker to Guinie... 1562," in Richard Hakluyt, The Principal Navigations, Voyages and Discoveries of the English Nation. (London, 1589), p. 132.

[25] Kenneth M. Stampp. The Peculiar Institution. (New York: Alfred A. Knopf. 1969). pp. 44-46.

mentality reflects through words, actions, and deeds, that the black man was a species of property that was incapable of being assimilated into the mainstream of American life. George M. Fredrickson is indeed perceptive in stating that the question of racism was grounded in a perceived fact of nature and that it would remain in an embryonic stage for years to come. Thomas Jefferson, as Fredrickson noted, as a chief spokesman for the American Enlightenment, was also frustrated and baffled by the question and burden of race, and obviously, suggested that the final judgment on the question be suspended until additional facts are available.[26]

Chattel slavery in the United States was, at least. a brutal, inhumane system. a crime against humanity, and a testimony to the evil capabilities of civilized man. This stance finds defense in the thoughts of such scholars as Carter G. Woodson, Eugene Genovese, E. Franklin Frazier. Gayraud S. Wilmore and Gilbert Osofsky, to mention a few. Carter Woodson stated succinctly that "the slaves were treated more like brutes subjected to a process known as "breaking in." Genovese stated that "cruel, unjust, exploitative, oppressive, slavery bound two peoples together in bitter antagonism ..." Frazier was more specific in his assessment of the horrors of slavery in his references to the initial capture (or purchase) of the slave on the coast of West Africa and their eventual transport to the New World. He refers to

---

[26] George M. Fredrickson. The Black Image in the White Mind. (New York: Harper A Row Publishers. 1971). pp. 1 -2.

the barracoons (concentration camps) where slaves were kept until there was an adequate load of human cargo for the ships. He cites the total disregard for human decency in the treatment of the slaves. There was no regard for sexual differences, tribal grouping, or family affiliations. In preparation for the "middle passage", "The Negroes were packed spoon-fashion in the slave ships, where no regard was shown for sex or age difference ..." Wilmore, quoting from the notes and sermons of the Reverend James Ramsay, a slaveholding preacher himself, refers to the expressions of Ramsay's personal positions on the horrors and antithetical realities of slavery: "Master and slave are in every respect opposite terms; the persons to whom they are applied, are natural enemies to each other. Slavery, in the manner and degree, that it exists in our colonies, could never have been intended for the social state; for it supposes tyranny on one side, treachery and cunning on the other. Nor is it necessary to discuss which gives the first occasion to the other."[27] Gilbert Osofsky, without hesitation, in the initial pages of his book, bluntly defines and describes the slave system as "a brutal, brutalizing, and alluring institution ...which in every aspect of the slave regime attempted to obliterate the slaves being."

Finally, what must be kept in mind are the words of Henry F. May that "obviously Negroes were not among those for whom opportunity must be preserved; their

---

[27] E. Franklin Frazier and C. Eric Lincoln. The Negro Church in America and The Black Church Since Frazier (New York: Schocken Books. 1974). pp. 9-11.

road was blocked not by corrupted interest but by the caste system." Very early in the American experience there began the decimation of racial barriers, based solely upon the color that would begin the ugliest chapter of our history. It is a history written with the blood extracted from the veins of thousands of black slaves who were penalized for racial reasons over which they had no control. Yes, America exploited people's labor and degraded them by insisting that the God of nature and nature's God had specifically created the black man inferior for the eternal purpose of bondage and servitude to the "superior" white race.

THE SLAVE COMMUNITY

From dawn to dusk the involvement in chores and errands on behalf of the master's vested interest was the typical daily lot of the slave.[28] He was expected to be at the complete disposal of the master, the slave driver, or the overseer. The slave, like any other piece of chattel, was expected and demanded to be a productive piece of property. But there were times when, and a place where, the slave master had given to him a degree of freedom to recline, relax and reflect. This was usually during the evening time after the daily chores and errands were well accomplished. The place to which the slave could resort was the slave quarters or the slave community.

---

[28] Henry F. May. The End of American Innocence. (New York: Alfred A. Knopf, 1959), pp. 20-24.

The slave quarters, it is noteworthy, were housing areas built specifically for the slaves.

The slave quarters were the centers of the slave community; however, the slave community encompassed a much broader perspective and wider horizon than simply the spatial limitations of the slave quarters. In a sense, the slave community was the plantation and the total environment in which the slave lived, moved, and realized his personhood, or the lack thereof. The purpose here is to concentrate upon slave life and behavior in the slave community as an approach to ascertaining the emergence of the undergirding principles upon which the slave developed his concept of freedom. What were the lifestyles in the slave community, the conversations, the social intercourses, the political ambitions, arid the religious convictions that permeated the community?[29]

John W. Blassingame, Leslie Howard Owens, Albert J. Raboteau, Thomas L. Webber, and E. Franklin Frazier, to mention a few, are perhaps the leading scholars on the subject, "The Slave Community in America." However, to understand the slave quarters as a place of total freedom from the watchful eye of the master and overseer is to misunderstand the ubiquitous and ever-present nature of the slave master's proximity to the slave quarters. The master was careful in strategically locating the slave quarters within eye-view of the "Big House" where the slave's movements and behavior could easily

---

[29] Kenneth M. Stampp. The Peculiar institution (New York: Alfred A. Knopf. 1969), pp. 3-4

be monitored and controlled. The slave quarters were usually located well within the sight and hearing range of the master and his hired overseer. A slave's personal testimony to the location of the quarters, and the internal and external construction as they appeared on a larger plantation provides some feeling for the living conditions to which the slave was subjected: "The houses that the slaves lived in were all built in a row, away from the big house. Just at the head of the street and between the cabins and the big house, stood the overseer's house. There were some forty or fifty of these two-room cabins facing each other across an open space for a street. In them, we lived. There was not much furniture. Just beds and a table and some stools or boxes to sit on. Each house had a big fireplace for heat and cooking."

It must be kept in mind that the primal purpose of the plantation and the slave quarters was not the comfort and pleasure of the slave. Accordingly, their construction anal furnishings reflected the bare minimum of comfort that gave the slave a place to sleep in preparation for another day's toiling in the fields of the plantation.[30] John Hope Franklin has rightly stated that ... "The primary concern of the owner was to get the world out of his slaves."

While the slave quarters were not an ideal place of beauty, and comfort, with elaborate furnishings, they were a place of retreat from the horrors experienced from dawn to dusk each day. Although proximity

---

[30] Leslie Howard Owens. This Species of Property. (New York: Oxford University Press, 1976), pp. 136-138.

placed the slave quarters within the eye-view of both the master and the overseer, there was an amazing development occurring literally under the noses of the symbols of power and humiliation: the slave developed his religion, politics, and social life. These aspects of his life had enormous possibilities for his existential situation and for his future freedom. Within the confines of the slave quarters and the parameters of the plantation, the slave utilized his limited time and creative resources to conceive, formulate, design, and effectuate a procedure whose ultimate goal was the reality of freedom. The logical question is perhaps, what set of dynamics was operative within the slave quarters that shifted the slaves' focus from the present reality of slavery to the possibility of liberation and total freedom?

Within the boundary of the slave quarters there developed among the slave a relatively sophisticated level of social stratification. E. Franklin Frazier historically introduced the idea and has very strongly defended the position that there developed within the slave community the "Invisible Institution", the forerunner of the Black Church in America.[31] Since the forms of social interactions between the slaves were limited to the predilection of the master, the social groupings, numbers, and places of congregating were not of the slave's own choosing. The number of slaves allowed to congregate was determined by the master; his workday was at the master's discretion, and his

---

[31] John Hope Franklin. From Slavery to Freedom. (New York: Alfred A. Knopf, 1976), p. 190.

social pleasures were to reach their peak between dusk and dawn. However, the time between dusk and dawn was the time for the slave to reflect upon his lot. Frazier posits that it was the "Invisible Institution' that granted the slave community a forum to develop the social cohesiveness needed for survival.

The plantation served as a place of physical detention without the aid of literal nails. However, there did exist an ever-presence of those invisible walls personified in the overseer. The overseer and the master always insisted that the presence of authority and control was always available. But when the slave resorted to the semi-privacy of the slave quarters, he used these valuable moments to devise plans for both his immediate and distant futures. The major and primary preoccupation of the slave was freedom. This preoccupation followed him to the fields, to the big house, and lived with him in the slave cabins.[32] The slave found a degree of hope and rays of light for the future in the Christian religion. John Blassingame asserts that by 1860 a large number of slaves had been exposed to the Christian religion through the Protestant missionary efforts. While their efforts to expose the slave to the Christian faith and to provide him with the rudiments of education were hampered by the slave system, the slave was able to absorb the basic tenets of the faith.

---

[32] E. Franklin Frazier and C. Eric Lincoln. <u>The Negro Church in America and The Black Church Since Frazier</u>. (New York: Schocken Books, 1974), pp. 21-24.

This faith would prove invaluable for the future freedom of the slave."

If from dawn to dusk was the principal agricultural production time for the slave master, then from dusk to dawn was the principal production time for the slave. From dusk to dawn was a significant time in the slave quarters. Within the slave, cabins developed a set of principles that encompassed the totality of slave existence. While the master lumped them together in close quarters with inadequate space for comfort and privacy, nonetheless the slaves' religious, social and political horizons continued to expand. On the plantation, in the slave quarters, and in the slaves' cabins were born the songs, folklore, religion, the tactics that would lead to their freedom.[33] While sports, fishing, hunting, and visiting relatives on nearby plantations consumed many of the slaves' leisure, his leisure time was not totally void of the urge and desire for freedom. Leisure time provided the slave the opportunity to think, reflect, strengthen family ties, and plan stratagems. Both John Blassingame and Kenneth Stampp have focused on the limitations placed upon the Negro by the slave system: the exclusion from the mainstream society, and the exposure to that brand of Christianity that was conducive to enhancing docility and agricultural productivity. The slave, robbed of his African culture arid prevented from practicing his native religion, was forced to live on the edges of society. The locations of the

---

[33] John W. Blassingame. The Slave Community (New York: Oxford University Press, 1979), pp. 311-312.

slave cabins. off the main thoroughfares, on the sides of the back roads, further, attest to the obvious attempts to isolate the slaves and relegate them to the edges of life. Although of a meager existence. and constructed of the most inferior quality of materials, the dynamics that were at work in the cabins between dusk and dawn have far-reaching implications for the slaves' freedom.

The logical question is, "...in what activities did the slaves engage between dusk and dawn?" In addition to dancing, drinking, telling tales, courting, and eating, there was an element of the cabin community whose insatiable desire was total freedom. It was in the cabin where the tale of Brier Rabbit" developed. This tale pits a weaker opponent, the slave, against the much stronger opponent, the master. This tale is an insidious approach, designed by the slave that attests to the crafty and wily capabilities of the slave. The crux of the slave's preoccupation was immediate survival and future freedom from the slave system. The close-knit nature of the slave cabin provided an environment conclusive to planning for those realities to materialize. Therefore. the family groupings, the religious gatherings, and the clandestine meetings were not totally given to fun and frivolity, but were occasions for planning and formulating means of escape from the slave system.

Melville J. Herskovits has noted, what seems to be, the relatively strong kinship ties that existed in the West African culture, and attests that a degree of the cultural norms persisted in the New World of the United States of America. He cites the composition of the relationship groupings in the African immediate family: "... the father, his wife, and their children., as a part of a larger unit." The close kinship groupings indigenous to West Africa formed a point of departure and a foundation for devising greater bonds that eventually included the freedom struggle. The zeal for freedom was born on the coast of their homeland, nurtured on the slave ships, further nourished on the plantation, and finalized in the slave cabins during conversations and religious worship. A key aspect of slave gatherings was the freedom available to them from dusk to dawn. Within the slave, cabins were where the stratagems were conceived and formulated. The attitudes of the master toward the slave necessitated craftiness on the part of the slave. Therefore, to avoid having secret stratagems revealed, there emerged among the slave a unique codified manner of communication. The slave had long known that his survival was heavily contingent upon his slyness; and, thus there emerged a number of behaviors that were specifically expressed that sent deliberately unclear and mixed signals to the slave master.

John W. Blassingame mentions three basic stereotypical slave characters: Sambo, Jack, and Nat. Jack reflected a slave who as long as he was fed, worked hard. Jack realized the unbalance of power and did what he deemed appropriate for his survival. Nat represents a slave who was keenly aware of the evils of the system and utilized all his time, intelligence, and power to destroy the system. Nat was radical, violent, uncooperative, and justified his actions by resorting to a divine mandate. Sambo reflected the slave who had no desire for freedom. He had made himself satisfied with the status quo. He was a "clown, an uncle 'Tom, an Uncle Remus, and very docile." The freedom struggles was born in the minds and actions of such stereotypes as Jack, Nat, and Sambo. Jack concealed his personal feelings and ambitions by overtly supporting the system on the one hand, and on the other hand, covertly abhorring disdain and hoping for its abrupt death. Nat utilized the basic tenets of the master's ethics, morality, and religion to authenticate the master's inhumanity. The Nat stereotype was somewhat of a "Jack-of-all-trades, to include being a field hand and a religious exhorter."[34]

The Sambo stereotype was, perhaps, operative in each stereotype at various times and under various conditions. Sambo appeared docile, cooperative, and happy. but Sambo was also a manipulator. Sambo laughed when there was not anything funny, said yes when it was no, said no when it was yes, scratched his head when it did not itch and appeared happy when internally he was torn apart. Sambo was not a fighter, he simply wanted to survive and, did what he knew the master wanted him to do. The words of the slave, Charlie Davis, is conveyed the image of Sambo: "Boss, I is kinda glad I is a black man, 'cause, you know, dere ain't much expected of dem nohow, and dat, by itself, takes a big and heavy burden off deir shoulders." On the back cover of John W. Blassingame's Slave Testimony is also an interesting letter written to Mr. William Riley of

---

[34] John W. Blassingame. The Slave Community. (New York: Oxford University Press, 1979), pp. 147-148.

Springfield, Kentucky, by Jackson Whitney, in which he stated: "I did all that was honorable and right while I was with you. although I was a slave. I pretended all the time that I thought you, or someone else had a better right to me than I had to myself, which you know is rather hard thinking."

While the Negro disguised his true feelings and played the role of a person who felt that his self-evaluation rendered him less than the master, it must be understood that these were survival tactics, and were not necessarily the internal feelings of the slave. The slave even pretended. to some degree, to adopt the religion of the master as an overt gesture of his assimilation and as identifying with his master's behest.[35] However, what the master did not fully understand was that the slave never totally identified with the master's religion, nor with a God who countenanced slavery under the umbrella of Christianity. Albert J. Raboteau refers to the inconsistency between slavery and Christianity in an incident of the brutality of Henry Bibb who was threatened with five hundred lashes for attending a prayer meeting. What is so ironic is that the master and brutalized was "... a deacon in the local Baptist church." Both Melville J. Herskovits and Herbert Aptheker were of the persuasion that had the slaves adopted the "white man's views and had lost their consciousness of group identity along with their African cultural background," the slave revolts never would have

---

[35] James Mellon, ed. Bullwhip Days. (New York: Weidenfold Nicoloon, 1988), pp. 457-458.

taken place. The Negro revalued a significant quantity of his African heritage and culture in the New World and those aspects of his Native culture that spoke to his needs, given the situation of slavery, he incorporated it into the struggle for freedom. Freedman and fugitive slaves testify that prior to the Civil War, the slave community had developed an extensive and relevant religious life apart from the master's religion. As E. Franklin Frazier has so forcefully articulated, one of the most significant developments among the slaves was the "Invisible Institution", the brush arbors, or hush arbors.[36] The slaves were rather discriminating and selected those tenets of Christianity that posed for them some significance and included them in their own religious confession. While the slave might have worshipped with the master on Sunday mornings, he, nonetheless, superseded Sunday morning with the clandestine, illicit worship practiced on weeknights and on Sunday nights in the slave cabins. Blassingame is rather specific that "a communalism born of oppression led to an emphasis on mutual cooperation, joyful camaraderie, humor, respect for elders, and an undisguised zest for life." It was the slaves' religious faith that provided the courage to defy the power of the masters. The slave cabins, hush arbors, and other meeting places afforded the slave an unusual amount of freedom. Within the slave cabins, the slave was able to escape the constant eye of the master; there he could think about his condition, practice his relation,

---

[36] Albert J. Raboteau. Slave Religion. (New York: Oxford University Press, 1978), pp. 214-215

and plan for his freedom. There developed within the slave cabins the songs, folklore, tales, sermons, and other means of escape. It has long been known that the slave housed his escape plan in codified language, symbols, and signs. James Cone, along with a long list of scholars, has noted the nature of the Negro spirituals and the insidious and codified messages they convey. In the Negro's prayers, in his worship and singing traditions were subdued feelings, hurts, pains, and a hope that far exceeded his present situation of slavery.[37] Slavery was a present reality, but freedom was a future hope. Therefore, it was in the words of such Negro spirituals that one gets the true sense of the slaves' inner feelings and aspirations:

> "Got one mind for white folks to see not needed another for what I know is me; He don't know, he don't know my mind, When he see me laughing Just laughing to keep front crying."

The Exodus story as is recorded in the Old Testament of the Holy Bible was the slaves' point of departure on the subject of freedom and liberation. The slave saw in that story the power of an omnipotent God who was always on the side of the weak, the poor, the deprived, and the enslaved. Thus, it was common for many of the slaves' codes for secret meetings, plans for escape, and revolutionary stratagems to reflect the destruction of the Pharaoh's army in the Red Sea. There seems to have

---

[37] John W. Blassingame. <u>The Slave Community</u>. (New York: Oxford University Press, 1979), pp. 128-134.

been the prevailing idea in the slave mentality that the master would understand the Exodus experience as rather anachronistic for the eighteenth and nineteenth-centuries, and totally irrelevant to both the slaves' lot and the master's destruction. The steal-away songs and themes were composed in the slave cabins and during the unique worship experiences of the slave as a codified message to inform other slaves of the next meeting. In the words of a former slave, Wash Wilson, are found the true essence and impact of the codified language of the slave community as preparations were made for secret meetings in the "Invisible Institution": "When de niggers go round singin' Steal Away to Jesus, dat mean dere gwine be a ligious meetin' dat night." De master ... didn't like dent religious meetin', so us natcherly slips off at night, down in de bottoms or somewhere; Sometimes us sing and pray all night."

Slave religion, or the religion of the slave, and black religion, or religion participated in by the slave have been the subject of much discussion, given many definitions, and branded as a simple black protest with revolutionary tendencies for generations.[38] They have been seen as attempts to exploit the Biblical norms for one's advantage, and rob the Bible of its true and original meanings. Black religion is essentially protested, but it is not limited simply to protest. Black religion, as seen in African culture, was a protest against the inherent evils perceived to permeate African society.

---

[38] James H. Cone. <u>God of the Oppressed</u>, (New York: The Seabury Press, 1975), pp. 23-25

The religious fervor of West Africa is well documented by the Anthropologist Melville Herskovits, who takes issue with Mecklin and Reuter, by positing that before the onslaught of American slavery there had developed a rather sophisticated religious and family life in West Africa. Herskovits further states that the rejection of the slave master's religion by the slaves contributed to the slave revolts. Those who brand black religion as simply black protest has limited views of black religion. While black religion is a protest against every form of slavery and injustice in this world, it is not solely limited to this-worldly interests.[39] Black religion is the most important product to be conceived, designed, developed, articulated, and utilized by the black community in the liberation struggle. The intriguing aspect of black religion is that it is uniquely black. It is a product of the slave cabins, slave plantations, and hush arbors; it is the result of the existential situation of an oppressed people who were able to find in the Holy Bible a ray of hope by resorting to the previous act of "An Almighty Sovereign God, who takes sides with the weak," as James Cone says. Black religion is a protest, a protest begun on the shores of Africa and kept alive until the Emancipation Proclamation became a reality. Black religion includes the cultural norms and experiences of the oppressed and community society.

It was inevitable, therefore, that much of black religion reflects incidents of protest. In the slave

---

[39] Rawick, ed. The American Slave: A Composite Autobiography. Vol. 5, Texas Narratives, pt. 4, p. 198.

community, perhaps the most important person was the black preacher; it was he who had a better education, charisma, and a more in-depth understanding of the divine mandate for freedom than the average field hand. It is a small wonder that out of the ranks of the slave preachers emerged the noted protest leaders: Nat Turner, Gabriel Prosser, Lott Carey, Henry Highland Garnet, and David Walker. Hence, the present writer posits that the protest aspect of black religion was not adopted from the white church. but emerged out of the black experience.[40]

---

[40] Cecil Wayne Cone. The Identity Crisis in Black Theology. (Nashville, Tennessee: African Methodist Episcopal Church Publishing, 1975), pp. 58-59.

CHAPTER III

THE SLAVE'S SURVIVAL OF SLAVERY

The slave developed phenomenal coping skills, mannerisms, and stereotypes as means of survival. One of the most common and familiar stereotypes was that of the Sambo image and accompanying behavior. At times the Sambo stereotype allowed for an appearance of happiness, docility a cooperative while at other times it allowed him to be a manipulator, he laughed when nothing was funny, he scratched his head when it was not itching and he said yes when it was no. Sambo was not a fighter, he just wanted to survive. In the words of Charles Davis: "Boss, I is kind of glad I is a black man, cause, you know, deer aint't much expected of dem no how, and dat, by itself, takes a bis and heavy burden off deir shoulders." Ibid., pp. 146-148.

It is safe to posit that the one continual cry and total obsession of the slave was total liberation and the freedom to live out, like other Americans, the ideals captured in the Declaration of Independence and in the magnificent words of the Constitution, which when realized, would have made for a "More Perfect Union." However, because of the delayed fruition of the ideas not becoming a reality for all, it was necessary for the development of the Liberation and Freedom movements. Reflects on one basic Institution that played a significant role in the Black liberation struggles: the Black Church. He points out that for the most part many of the revolutionary leaders had connections to both the visible and the invisible church and that they responded out of significant religious convictions. Classic examples of those religious connections were expressed in both the behaviors of Nat Turner and David Walker.

The religion of the slave became one of the most potent weapons for change of status in a socially hostile environment. There was within the religion of the slave a blatant refusal to dichotomize the this-worldly from the other-worldly, rather the slave saw and understood his religion as having significant implications for both worlds. Therefore, the slave was cautious not to become so other-worldly that he became no earthly good. While the slave master strove to convince the slave that his eternal reward was in the beyond, the slave understood that freedom in this world was not only a constitutional right provided but a divine right given to all men, rather than given by the state and thus capable of being taken away. Within the slave community, there was a blending together of biblical themes that had as their core liberation. Therefore, the theological positions that rendered the slave as inferior, whether preached by the Bishop of London or the slave master, had very little effect on producing a model slave. Within the theology of the slave was the continual conviction that freedom was a divine-human enterprise as is reflected in the beliefs of a slave:

> "He have been wid us, Jesus, He still wid us, Jesus. He still wid us, Jesus. He will be wid us, Jesus, Be Wid us to the end or I been preaching the Gospel and farmin' since slavery time when I starts Preaching I couldn't read or write and had to preach. What massa told me but I knowed there's something better for them, but tell them I kept on the sly. That I Done lots. I tell lem iffen they keeps pray in' the Lord Will set them free."[41]

Inevitably, the question arose as to how could it be possible for the God of the white slave master to be the same God as the black slave. For the slave, this was not an easy question to answer. A God who sanctioned slavery and brutal physical abuse was not possibly the God of the slave who countenanced slavery under the umbrella of Christianity. Albert J. Raboteau refers to this inconsistency between Christianity and slavery and points out an incident of brutality in the slave life of one, Henry Bibb who was beaten with hundreds of stripes for attending a prayer meeting. However, what is so ironic is that the slave master was a deacon in the local Baptist church. Albert J. Raboteau. Slave Religion. (New York: Oxford University Press, 1978) pp. 214-215.[42] Both

---

[41] Albert J. Raboteau. Slave Religion. (New York: Oxford

[42] Albert J. Raboteau in Slave Religion. (New York: Oxford University Press. 1978), p.215.

Melville J. Herskovits and Herbert Aptheker was of the persuasion that had the slaves fully adopted the white man's religion they would have lost their group identity and their African cultural background, thus never becoming active in the slave revolts. Anthropologically, the slave retained his African identity, his religion, and his culture even in disguise. As E. Franklin Frazier has so forcefully articulated, one of the most significant developments among the slave was the "invisible institution", the brush arbors, or hush arbors. Thus, while the slave was forced, quite often, to worship with the master -in the master's church-on Sunday mornings, he nonetheless superseded Sunday morning with his clandestine, illicit worship he practiced on weekends and Sunday nights in the slave cabins, in hush arbors and down by the riversides.[43] One of the greatest and most profound voices that lent support to the Liberation Movement was of one, Bishop Richard Allen. Allen who emerged from virtual obscurity as a slave in the State of Delaware and one who rose to religious and social prominence in the State of Pennsylvania is a life that is synonymous with protest and freedom. It is unthinkable, given the history of his later life, that Allen was a docile slave who never spoke out against slavery. Thus, Allen's protest efforts rose to a A new level in November 1787 during a worship service at St. George Methodist Episcopal Church in Philadelphia, Pennsylvania when

---

[43] Carol V. R. George. Segregated Sabbaths: Richard Allen and the Emergence of Independent Black Churches. (New York: Oxford University Press, 1973), pp.21-23.

Allen and Absalom Jones were ejected from the church. St. George was a church where blacks and whites were allowed to worship together, however, blacks sat in the galleries. The gallery seating was caused because the number of blacks increased; therefore, a new policy was instituted relegating blacks to the galleries. But Allen and Jones gradually gravitated towards the front and commenced to make loud noises during prayer time. Consequently, while on their knees they were approached by a trustee and forced off their knees, and were told, "You must not kneel here...you must get up." The incident at St. George catapulted Allen into the limelight of religious history. Historically, from this incident comes into existence the African Methodist Church and vocal voice for freedom and liberation in the United States of America 21 The incident at St. George Church not only reveals Allen's commitment to the religious faith embraced in Methodism but also his new and invigorating commitment to liberation. It has been long established that religion played a significant role in black liberation. It is interesting that while the slave master read in the Bible support for the subjugation of blacks to slavery while the slave read the same Bible and saw grounds for liberation. The Exodus story and the liberation of the Jews was biblical precedent for the liberation of the slaves. Allen was initiated while living on the Stokeley farm during the time of a visiting Methodist circuit rider's revival during which Allen's life took a radical turn towards religion. It was the tenets of Methodism that expressed emphasis on personal conversion and individual responsibilities that altered

Allen's life and direction. Thus, the remainder of Allen's life was to reflect these tenets of his religious faith and led him to his stance against slavery. Methodism, historically, had taken a position against slavery and had set forth in the Methodist Discipline an attack on the slave institution. Allen's companion, Absalom Jones, confessed later that the incident in St. George by Allen and his companions was a prophetic protest against segregated worship. This firm conviction of Allen moved him to oppose slavery and to speak out against social-injustice which distinguished him as one of the earliest champions of social justice during the nineteenth-century. Not only was Richard Allen instrumental in the final break of blacks from white churches, but he was also a leader of great influence in the Free African Society. Allen's preoccupation was separation was the separation of blacks from the white church. Allen's zeal for separation, coupled with a quest for Negro identity, led to aggressive efforts to purchase property and to build a church building that was to become dominated and led by blacks. Allen conceived the black church as a power base, and his idea led to the reality that the only institution owned and controlled by blacks in the United States is the Black Church. It was the religious and social freedom inherent within Allen's idea of physical, religious, and political separation that later influenced another civil rights champion, David Walker. Allen, as did many of his contemporaries, sought to force America to live up to its ideals as are expressed in the Declaration of Independence and the Preamble to the Constitution. However, most American blacks knew that they were not included in those high-flown ideals concerning "all men," as was enunciated in the Declaration of Independence. This reality was reinforced by custom, practice, and by judicial decisions, as in Plessey v Ferguson. To further ensure physical separation and to further emphasize the assumption of color-superiority, there were developed institutional patterns, local laws, and codes to further define the blacks as property or three-fifths of a man for the purpose of determining legislative representation. It was the fact that the Church acquiesced to that constitutional violation that presents an anomaly. To rationalize the Church's acquiescence to a societal matter, the slavocracy tended to shift the slave's focus from this world to the heavenly kingdom and, thus, the slave master became involved in efforts that fitted the slave for living in his dehumanized conditions here on earth. Therefore, asserting further those blacks were less than human beings in this world. This level of mentality tended to arise out of the general agreement with the Roman Catholic Chief Justice Roger B. Taney decision of 1857, a decision that rendered the slave a subordinate to his master. Taney further stated, in essence, that "the slaves had no rights which white men had an obligation to respect." Noteworthy is that this decision was rendered, not form the back woods of rural America but from the highest Court of the Nation. This decision strongly suggests either a blatant disregard for the Declaration of Independence and the Constitution or a denial of the inherent equal worth of the slave; the latter seems to be true. Therefore, with this level of social and legal mentality pervading, the only means of achieving liberation and freedom was acquiescence or civil disobedience. The latter was the most effective!

Joining the ranks alongside Allen were two additional voices, the Reverend Nathaniel Paul and David Walker. As has been alluded to previously in this presentation, religion played a significant role in the liberation struggles of the slave. The Black church was born on and out of the frontier of protest and she has never forgotten the nature of her origin and mission. In the slave quarters, away from the watchful eyes of the slave master, she chartered a course that would eventually lead to liberation and freedom. While there were, unquestionably, large numbers of persons who were instrumental in the quest for freedom of slaves, the black preacher stood as an unmovable symbol of God's presence in the struggle. The nature of the black preacher's sermons was of a revolutionary fervor that corralled the slave to action. Black people needed the preacher because of his insights into divinity and his natural wit. Therefore, they relied on him to steer them clearly and safely through the turbulent waters of the slave system to better days ahead[44]. The Reverend Nathaniel Paul conceptualized the nature and purpose of the Liberation struggle and utilized his "God-given insights" to rid the Nation of its worst sin, slavery!

Reverend Paul understood freedom as a priceless, God-ordained gift, and therefore, was worth fighting for even at the cost of physical death. The core of the

---

[44] Gayraud s. Wilmore. <u>Black Religion and Black Radicalism</u>. (Garden City: Doubleday and Company, Inc., 1972), p. 2.

concept of freedom that pervaded the period, 1755-1800, was based on the slaves' understanding of the natural rights of man. Richard Allen was a southerner by birth, but the struggle for freedom of the slaves was not limited to any one geographical location of the slave, it was the concern of the slave wherever one slave lived. Thus, the joining of Reverend Nathaniel Paul and Reverend Richard Allen reflects the universal concern for liberation. The Reverend Nathaniel Paul was a native of New York. Born in the city of Albany, New York in 1755, where he served as pastor of the African Baptist church. Nathaniel was so committed to the Freedom struggle that he resigned from his pastoral assignment and became fully involved in the liberation struggle. Paul is most famously known for his famous address given in 1827, entitled: "An address delivered on the celebration of the Abolition of Slavery in the State of New York." Thus, Paul became one of the earliest pioneers of the ant-slavery efforts in the United States[45] Nathaniel Paul's concept of freedom was one that was inconsistent with the social norms of the Eighteenth and Nineteenth centuries of American life: half slave and half free. While this was the social phenomenon of the period, Paul saw a grave inconsistency between the ideas and the ideals of the Declaration of Independence and the preamble to the Constitution. Out of the inconsistency of the social phenomena, Reverend Paul arrived at what

---

[45] Henry Clay Bruce. The New Man: Twenty-Nine Years as a Slave, Twenty-Nine Years as a Free Man. (York, Pennsylvania: Anstadt Press, 1895), p. 73.

he understood as sin. Sin, for Paul, was disobedience to God's will for the freedom of all peoples. For Paul, this presents the question of the inconsistency between God and slavery. Therefore, Paul's continual rhetorical question was "Why are black people living in slavery and perpetual servitude?" Obviously, there were questions Paul could have answered himself rather than seeking to dialogue with his God. But he chose, rather, to seek engagement with his God as is seen in the following as he raises questions in one of his typical dialogues with his God:

> "And, oh thou immaculate God, be not angry with us While we come into this thy sanctuary and make the bold inquiry in this thy holy temple, why it was that thou didst look on with calm indifference of an unconcerned spectator, when thy holy law was violated, Carter G. Woodson. [24]Negro Orators and Their Orations. (Washington, D. C.: Associated Publishers, 1925), p. 69.

Thy divine authority despised and a portion of thine own creatures reduced to a state of mere vassalage and Misery?"

Herein lies the sum total of Paul's concept of freedom. Paul espoused the position that a sovereign God who is righteous would not allow perpetual slavery but that He would eventually bring about freedom for the slaves.[46] While Bishop Richard Allen and the Reverend Nathaniel

---

[46] Carter G. Woodson. Negro Orators and Their Orations. (Washington, D. C.: Associated Publishers, 1925), p. 69.

Paul mounted serious efforts to rid America of slavery, they were also joined in the struggle by a David Walker. David Walker did not emerge from the rank of the clergy, rather, he was a person of strong social convictions and a strong advocate of the freedom of the slave. Walker was a native North Carolinian who also harbored a disdain for slavery. Walker was born in Wilmington, North, and Carolina in 1785 during the highest of chattel slavery. While Walker's writings are limited, his most powerful and attention-getting article is known as <u>David Walker's Appeal</u>, appearing in1829. The Appeal sets forth Walker's concepts of God, his theology, and his history of social justice and racial equality. The Appeal reveals, Walker's abhorrence of the inconsistency between the American slave system, the Declaration of Independence, and the Constitution. David Walker expresses his disdain for the Declaration and the Constitution as did Supreme Court Justice Thurgood Marshall 125 years later: "... that the Constitution was flawed and that he saw little wisdom or foresight in the Framers." While Justice Marshall saw little foresight, Thomas Jefferson saw the Framers as demigods or as extraordinary men of wisdom and insights.[47] However, in spite of the obvious inconsistencies between the ideas of the Declaration of Independence, the Constitution, and the realities of the slave system, those who led the liberation struggle frequently referenced those documents as providing

---

[47] John P. Kaminski and Richard Leffler, eds. <u>Creating the Constitution</u>. (Madison, Wisconsin: The Center for the Study of the American Constitution, 1991), pp. vii-viii.

ideal lifestyles for all if implemented. But history reports a diametrically opposed reality. The reality of continual slavery provoked the writing of Abigail Adams in 1774 "It has always appeared a most iniquitous scheme to me to fight for ourselves for what we are daily robbing and plundering from those who have as good a right to freedom as we have." Strangely enough, Thomas Jefferson had written: "A Summary View of the Rights of British America" in which he stated that the abolition of slavery was the desire of the colonists, but that it had become difficult because Britain had blocked the efforts to stop the slave trade. Mrs. Adam's position against slavery was most powerful and thought-provoking, even though anti-establishment or the time. Professor John Hope Franklin entertains this idea at length in his work.[48] The era of David Walker was one of social upheaval and social change. It was a time of polarization between the slavocracy and the gradual developing sentiments toward freedom emerging from the Northern industrialized economy. While the southern economy rested largely on the relatively cheap labor force provided by slave labor and was thus an economic necessity; the north focused, to some degree, on social justice and racial equality. It is rather interesting to observe the theologies of the so-called mainline, High-Church churches and the theologies of the Black Church. Professor Reinhold Niebuhr speaks briefly to that issue

---

[48] John Hope Franklin. From Slavery to Freedom: A History of Negro Americans. (New York: Random House, 1969}, pp. 128-129, 138-139.

in his assessment of those positions when he suggested that the social arrangements of slavery were God's way of keeping things in check and were ordained by "natural law." Niebuhr further indicates that the church understood slavery as a part of the Christian ideal. However, I tend to disagree with that position because it tended to offer evidence that individual Christians who manumitted their slaves suggest that the gospel had, simultaneously, both a positive and a negative impact on the slave mentality and behavior.[49] Needlessly to note, the level of biblical interpretation is diametrically opposed to the Christianity of the New Testament Bible. Noteworthy was the Old Testament understanding of and abhorrence of second-class human existence, as is seen in Job 3: 13-23. That text expresses disdain for chattel slavery in pre-Cristian literature.

David Walker moved from his native North Carolina to Boston, Massachusetts during the early 1820s where he began associating with learned men and later became identified with Richard Allen. As has been pointed out earlier in this paper, the Black Church played a significant role in the liberation struggle as understood from the relationship of Walker with Allen. In order to get a fuller sense of Allen's impact on the life of Walker one needs to feel the image of Allen in the mind of Walker as is seen in Article IV of Walker's Appeal, "I shall give an extract from that article of that truly Reverend Divine of Philadelphia..."

---

[49] Reinhold Niebuhr. Moral Man and Immoral Society. (New York; Charles Scribner's Sons, 1960), pp. 12, 76-77.

The church-relatedness comes out in Walker's sense of interdependence, the interconnectedness, and the interrelatedness between God and man. The literature suggests that Walker's admiration for Allen was almost like that of a god because he idolized him as truly Reverend Divine and continued to find resources in Allen's writings and speeches.[50] The socio-cultural milieu that produced a David Walker was of such that rendered on the one hand a slave and on the other hand another free was a tantalizing paradox for Walker and developed within Walker a disdain for the status quo. The blatant imbalance and the lack of equitable distribution of economic wealth led him to develop a revolutionary behavior that could only be satisfied when total equality was a reality. Strangely enough, Walker's concept of freedom emerges out of the Declaration of Independence and the Constitution of the United States. Ironically, slavery and customs were such that even the author of the Declaration of Independence did intend to have blacks included in those grandiose ideas of the Document. Martin E. Marty.

Pilgrims in Their Own Land: 500 Years of Religion in America. (New York: Penguin Books, 1984), pp. 165-166, 228-229. The Declaration could have been more specific and direct given the fact that by the time the document was drafted blacks had fought in wars in defense of the Colonies at Lexington, Concord, and at Bunker Hill. But even these patriotic soldiers were not even included in provisions of those "We hold these truths to be

---

[50] Freedom Journal, November 2, 1827. Vol 1, No. 34.

self-evident", nor were they a part of those inalienable rights to include life, liberty, and the pursuit of what the Framer considered as happiness for the drafter. What the slave wanted was whatever was included in the mind of the slave master as "all men are created equal...endowed by their creator..." It is noteworthy that at various junctures in history freedom has been exploited and utilized to destroy freedom. However, this concept of freedom is antithetical to the freedom that inherently implies to and involves social responsibility and ethical behavior. Thus, one's freedom to destroy freedom is tantamount to anarchy rather than social freedom. In a sense, the freedom which the slave sought was essentially the identical freedom for which the slave master sought nothing more nor less.

The ancient philosopher Plato taught that "... ideas are an eternal reality and that they cannot be eradicated, or changed." From the outset of this work there has been the focus on the institution of slavery and, essentially, the ideas responsible for its institution, promotion, and existence for much too long in the Nation's History. Contemporaneous with the promotion of Slavery were the Liberation Movements whose ultimate goals were to rid the Nation of its greatest sin. Obviously, the two most powerful and motivating foci have been, of course, the Declaration of Independence and the Constitution of the United States of America. While the initial statements of purposes of both documents are progressive concepts, however, the actualization has not yet been manifested in the history of the United States. World governments have never been so arrogant in defining the sole purpose and rationale for the formation of democracies or, democratic republics, as has been accentuated in "We the People, in order to form a more perfect union, establish justice (not for the few), ensure domestic tranquility, provide for the common defense, promote the general welfare, and secure the blessings of liberty to ourselves and our posterity, do ordain and establish this Constitution for the United States of America." "We hold these truths to be self-evident, that all men are created equal, that they are endowed by their Creator with certain unalienable Rights, that among these are Life, Liberty and the pursuit of Happiness." When one chooses to focus on the Declaration of Independence and the Constitution of the United States and to conduct a thorough examination in order to determine if the Ideas of those Documents have manifested into Ideals and realities for all Americans, one will arrive at a point of incredulity. The immortal words of the late Supreme Court Justice Thurgood Marshall stated some years ago that the Constitution was flawed and that he saw little wisdom or foresight in the minds of the Framers continue to cast doubt as to whether America is yet willing to live out the ideas and ideals of the world's two most precious documents. While Justice Marshall's statement is a rather alarming assessment of a Document that is held by many Americans as running a close second to the Holy Bible, Marshall was not alone in his assessment.

While Justice Marshall's assessment was of a critical nature and sent shock waves across the judicial horizon, it was much milder than some of the assessments of contemporary opponents and critics. The main group of opponents was the Antifederalists who argued that the current government under the Articles of Confederation need some fixing, while others claimed it was the result of a closed-door meeting held under the cloud of darkness. Of course, there was the further suggestion that "the evil genius of darkness presided over the Constitutional Convention at its birth and that every deceptive trick had been used so that it would appear that this "spurious brat was received as the genuine offspring of heaven-born liberty."[51] On June 11, 1776, Congress appointed a Committee of five persons to draft a document later known as the Declaration of Independence; although some never recognized the Document as a Declaration of Independence. Thus, the task of compiling a document that was to ultimately, in fact, document the political, social, economic, and human rights rationale for the separation of the Colonies from Great Britain. Needlessly to mention, the task was to involve a number of talents including the best minds available. Thomas Jefferson, Alexander Hamilton, John Adams, Benjamin Franklin, Roger Sherman, and Robert R. Livingston were appointed to draft the Document. Noticeably early on during the process Jefferson was selected to provide an original draft for the others to critique prior to the presentation to the Convention. The Committee was composed, of course,

---

[51] John P. Kaminski and Richard Leffler, eds. <u>Creating the Constitution</u>. (Madison Wisconsin: The Center for the Study of the American Constitution, 1991), pp. vii-viii

of men who were quite familiar with the histories of nations and governments which provided them with the necessary skills and insights to prepare them for the task. It is significant to understand that each of these men was chosen and appointed by Congress for such an unprecedented task never undertaken on the soil of the original colonists. It was, at least, a rather bold and courageous venture, taken with death lurking over their heads. However, June 11, 1776, will remain in American history as the day on which a new nation was born, and in the words of the drafters, "... dedicated to the proposition that all men are created equal..." The drafters of the Document were men of recognizable stature which enabled them to draw upon their educational, political, and cultural histories in meeting the challenges that lay ahead. Thomas Jefferson, an accomplished lawyer and statesman; Adams, an educated educator and also a statesman were the original signers while the remaining five were captured and tortured by British forces. Needlessly to say, with Jefferson's skills as a trained lawyer coupled with Adams's educational background the task was in good hands for the original presentation on June 28, 1776. Since its inception, the Document has been acclaimed as one of the greatest ever produced by humans and it stands today as a model ideal for humanity. However, while there were many admirers of the Document accepted at the Convention; there were also large numbers of opponents who would join with Justice Thurgood Marshall that the Framers showed very little insights and foresight in adopting a "flawed

Constitution." Therefore, it seems safe to posit that the "flaws" to which Justice Marshall referred in the Document and in the Constitution rest in, not only the lack of specificity of language but also in the obvious subsequent failure to recognize the equality of all peoples. Hypothetically, was there present in the mind of Marshall the fact that a segment of America upon whom the contents of the Document was to be imposed was not a part of the committee? Hence the Nation's Congress has continually sought to correct those oversights or the deliberate ignorance (ig-no- rance, or neglect) of human equality. Logically, if one fizzles before the finish, one was faulty from the start.

The present writer's position is that neither the drafters of the Declaration of Independence nor the Framers of the Constitution ever had in mind for the slave to be recognized as an equal person, and thus, they were never endowed by the State with certain inalienable rights of life, liberty and the pursuit of happiness as were their white counterparts. To further validate and actualize the sense of reality the slavocracy enacted laws, and codes and sought Biblical, biological, and social precedents to validate the slave master's assertion that the black slave was inherently inferior to the white person. On the whole, it was not very difficult for the political community to find support for promoting a human atrocity as long as there were pseudo-theologians who would find selected biblical texts to support an already conceived idea.

The biblical story of Israel's sojourn in Egypt was a classic for those Christians who needed validation to keep slaves. But what the preachers to the slaves failed to do was to read the whole story, God delivered Israel! Therefore, interestingly enough, the identical precedent that the white preacher employed to validate perpetual slavery was the very one that the slave employed to vindicate God's justice in the sense that God brought about total liberation of Israel from the slave conditions in Egypt. Nonetheless, there were those Christians who were bent on the issue of slavery that there developed a social and theological mentality that enabled support for the slave system; the following suggests such, "Slavery was good for the slave; the slave owners took on the burdens of caring for the interest of the inferior beings, seeing that they would be fed, clothed and given religious instruction." One might ask the rhetorical question, "from whence would have the food that fed both the slave and the slave owner have come had it not been for the slave's free labor"?

At the Constitutional Convention held in Richmond, Virginia in 1829, the discussion arose as to whether to abolish slavery in that state. Strangely enough, the answer came from Thomas Drew, President of the College of William and Mary, who argued that slavery was practiced in the Bible and that God himself had slaves and allowed Abraham, and his offspring to hold slaves. While that is true, he fails to mention the Year of Jubilee when all slaves were free and all debts were canceled. He also fails to mention the period of servitude or the seven years of servitude and freedom of the slave. Significantly, there might be some concern as to whether the preachers of the pro-slavery persuasion who select Biblical texts to support the slavery of blacks, tail to reference the Biblical incident in Second Kings Chapter 5: 1-27, with emphasis on verse 27, and provide a theological interpretation of that text. In Biblical studies, there are the terms pro-texting, or relating a number of non-related scriptures and superimposing your own meanings on them, and Biblicism, or adhering to the exact meaning of the texts and there is bifurcating, or splitting into two parts. The above-mentioned process seems to the present writer that the preacher to the slave owners said what the masters wanted to hear and ultimately what the master wanted the slave to hear, thus promoting further subjugation to the whims and policies of the slave masters. The seldom mentioned aspects of the difference between Biblical slavery and servitude and that of perpetual servitude in the United States are the denigration of the slave as being less than a human being which is a vast difference from that of Biblical servitude. The classic example of the Christian relationship to a servant is exemplified in Paul's letter Philemon (Philemon 1:16) is the paradigm. The significant difference between Biblical slavery was that while it served a specific there was a graduation date. Obviously, when juxtaposing the two historical systems one is able to distinguish the historical differences: a graduation date for one and perpetual slavery for the other! Thus, a relatively easily seen and understood difference!

The Drafters of the Declaration of Independence and the Framers of the Constitution were men of extraordinary skill and social, cultural, political, legal, and religious insights. Consequently, they were very much in touch with a variety of norms of the era and were fully aware of the outcome of the documents to which they were tasked to draft. Obviously, Jefferson was esteemed highly above his peers in the sense that he was chosen to do the initial draft work The other members of the Committee were also well abreast of the socio-political climate of the day therefore, why were not these voluminous reservoirs of knowledge called to the forefront and employed to speak specifically to the issues of not just freedom for "ourselves", but to articulates in certain terms, not just all men, rather, all peoples, regardless of race, creed, gender, color, religion or national origin. The intellectual genius of Thomas Jefferson, coupled with his Deistic religious identification, should have known that the God with whom he identified was not only a God who wound up the clock and that it has run for millions, and billions of years without failure would have been meticulous enough to make all men equal as is seen during the creation story of the Hebrew Bible, and to which it is attested in Acts 17: 24-27. It seems that the text needs very little interpretation. There does possibly exists the argument that the pro-slavery Christian might have overlooked these texts when defending the inferiority of the slave to the master class.

The Drafters of the Declaration of Independence were aware of the Rule of Law. Jefferson was keenly aware of the Four Universal Principles of law. Jefferson as an influential lawyer would have been well aware of accountability under the law; he would have known that the law is stable, just, and is to be applied evenly, and to protect the fundamental rights of all; he would have known the process by which laws are enacted, enforced fairly and efficiently; and he would have known that justice is to be delivered timely by competent and ethical persons.[52]

It is not alarming or surprising that a Nation that bases its faith on the God of the Bible would also reference a number of religious leaders and philosophical thinkers of the past in order to add credence and validity to its form of government, the United is a classic example. The frequency with which religious and philosophical terms are used in the Nations transactions: The Oath of Office, the signing of documents, the dates reflecting the Christian year, and A.D. on a number of business transactions. The above-mentioned realities suggest a nation deeply rooted in religious principles and values. The question is ultimately raised, "...if this is a religious Nation, then for what reason does the Nation's behavior differ in actual practice from the developed ideas and policies upon which She was ostensibly founded? Therefore, one is forced further to raise the question as to the difference between the ideas of the Declaration of Independence, "...we hold these truths to be self-evident that all men are created equal" the actualization of those ideas into reality for peoples.

---

[52] (https:/ worldjust iceproject. org/ about-us/ overview/ what- rule-law

The true understanding of the Declaration of Independence is that as is seen in the paragraph with the words: "We hold these truths to be self-evident." In philosophy, the term self-evident suggests empirical verification which is to be employed to enable one to verify or validate through or by the senses: the touch, the smell, the hearing, the tasting, and the seeing of realities. Understandably, one does not need an explanation if verified by the senses because one knows when one feels, smells, hears, tastes, and sees. Thus, one is able to know what is happening to her through sense perceptions. For the person to whom the phenomenon is occurring, it is reality while for the onlooker is mere perception. Thus, the slave would conceal his true self in order to survive the socio-cultural status endured in the hostile world of slavery. Sometimes he would laugh just to keep from crying.

The American Nation was not developed within a vacuum or without foreign examples and influences. The Nation's Constitution was modeled after a number of existing governments and constitutions of Europe. Jefferson and Adams were quite cosmopolitan in their political orientations. They were aware of the great thinkers of the past, Plato, Aristotle, John Locke, Kant, et cetera; they were also aware of and familiar with many of the religious thinkers of the past. The four men who, perhaps, exerted the most influence on the shaping of national thought were Benjamin Franklin, Thomas Jefferson, James Madison, and John Adams. Franklin was a great defender of federalism, a critic of parochialism, a great thinker, and a strong defender of religious liberty; Jefferson was a Virginia statesman, scientist, lawyer, and diplomat who chose to substitute "the pursuit of happiness" for "property" as is seen in John Locke's schedule of natural rights; the so-called "Father of the Constitution"; James Madison, a man of science, a politician and a diplomat; John Adams was also a statesman, diplomat whose political philosophy reflects a passion of reason, justice which nature has not limited. These were men of the American Enlightenment whose reservoirs of knowledge contributed greatly to the formation of the Nation's governmental formation. It is rather difficult to believe that they were not aware of the writings of Emanuel Kant whose Critique of Pure Reason spoke to the ethical principle set forth in his Categorical Imperative as being necessary for guiding human behavior. Therefore, conceivably, John Locke's political theory weighed heavily in the formation of both the Declaration of Independence and the Constitution of the United States; so heavily that he has been suggested as "...the philosophical founder of America."

CONCLUSION

The most difficult and incomprehensible chapter in the history of the United States of America is the chapter in which the history of American slavery is recorded. Slavery in the United States represents a relatively long period in American history- or in the history of America-because, the extent of brutality perpetrated upon the slave is not essentially women, Indians, and others. Literature, research, and extended studies validate what seems as an obvious disregard for certain segments of society. This work is not to accentuate the historically obvious; rather it is to further call attention to what has been and is, for all practical purposes, a continuing reality in America- "The home of the Free and the Land of the Brave." One can hardly raise the question: "are the Constitution and the Declaration of Independence flawless Documents?" Needlessly to say, historically, there are resounding YEAS from all corners of the Nation. Researchers and a number of provocative thinkers have spared no pain in pointing out to the Nation a large number of the greatest flaws of the Constitution of the United States; one of the flaws is the failure to include equal rights provisions for persons on the grounds of sexual and sex needs and the obvious flaw as relates to specifics in the race, ethnicity, women, cultural, social and cultural equality[53] the literature on the subject of whether the Nation has defaulted on

---

[53] https://www.quora.com/What-are-the-greatest-flaws-of-the-Constitution-of-the United-States, 8/1/2017.

Her The original promise is quite voluminous, and it strongly suggests the affirmative, yes! However, one may choose to remain focused on the past rather than on the mindset of two centuries ago and attempt to understand what was a cultural and racial climate that did not allow the Framers of the Documents under study to envision the political and social development of contemporary society.

While it is not easy for contemporary humanity to get into the minds of pre-twenty-first century thinkers, it seems safe to posit that the all created equal might have very easily implied Constitution; and additional literature that accentuates the potentials flaws of both Documents, it seems appropriate to offer suggests as to create actions that will facilitate speedy corrections. One such approach is the amendment to the Constitution provision; public outcry; change of local and state laws; intentional inclusion of minority studies in the curricula of education. However, these are minimal steps, however microscopic there is offered the effort to initiate change and thus growth. There is a strong belief in the heart of the present writer- that one might focus on the suggested steps, and there is the possibility that better race relations are possible. While one possibility is that the focus is only on blacks and other minorities; the concern is that all persons are ensured the ideals cited in the Documents referenced frequently above. The insights contained herein offer non-minorities a social-cultural perspective that enhances cultural understandings that facilitate a level of understanding of, and an appreciation for another perspective in human relations. But most importantly, the legal profession may choose to revisit the Constitution, detect its flaws, and offers amendments to correct them. After all, the Constitution is a continually growing Document.

CHAPTER IV

THE FREEDOM MOVEMENTS

Political, social, and economic freedom was an undiminished desire that was insatiable by the black existential situation of slavery. "Free indeed, free from death, free from hell, free from work, free from white folks, free from everything is, perhaps, a typical and an eternal aspiration of the slave."[54] The "Invisible Church" that held secret, public, and codified clandestine gatherings of black slaves, ostensibly for worship, had at the core of those gatherings liberation from systems, orders, ideologies, and white people that sought to render them as less than total persons.[55] Religion, as was imposed upon blacks by the white power structure, was inherently inconsistent with the slave's concept and structural understanding of religion and of their

---

[54] Eric Lincoln. The Black Experience in Religion. (Garden City, New York: Anchor Press/Doubleday, 1974), pp. 155-156.

[55] Henry Clay Bruce. The Now Nan: Twenty-nine Years as a Slave. (York, Pennsylvania: 1895), p. 73.

God.⁵⁶ A large number of slave masters were deeply religious and went to some extremes to ensure the religious education of the slaves. While this gesture would ultimately prove to be an invaluable asset to black freedom, the slave master had as a primary objective the docility of the slaves. The apparent motivation was that the religious education of the slave would render him a more manageable, productive, and valuable possession. However, the slave saw an inconsistency between his religion and the religion of the slave master. The missionaries supposed the slave master's religion, and there was a forced co-existence between Christianity and slavery that was quite appalling to most slaves and, therefore. was never fully accepted by the slaves.⁵⁷

At the core and forefront of black religion, or the religious expressions of black people was the pervading desire for deliverance from the dehumanization inevitably inherent within the slave system. Frazier might have touched the core of black thought and dream when he pointed out that the sacred folk songs express the awe and wonder of the Negro in regard to life and death "...and his desire to escape from the uncertainties and frustrations of this world."⁵⁸

The community in which the slaves lived was one perpetrated upon them by the slave master and was

---

⁵⁶ Albert J. Raboteau. Slave Religion. (New York: Oxford University Press, 1978), pp. 214-215.

⁵⁷ Thomas L. Webber. Deep Like the Rivers. (New York: Morton and Company. 1978), pp. 43-45.

⁵⁸ Franklin E. Frazier. The Negro Church in America. (New York: Schocken Books. 1976). p. 20.

accurately described as anything short of an ideal community if, in fact, community implies commonality, decision-making as to destiny, and self-determination. The religion of the slave is, in fact, a blatant protest against the slave master's efforts to impose upon him a religion whose Sunday morning exhortations were incongruous with the daily behavior of the slave master. Raboteau points out this in congruency: "Henry Bibb was threatened with five hundred lashes on the naked back for attending a prayer meeting... because he had no permission to do so." The white master who threatened Bibb with this punishment was, incidentally, a deacon of the local Baptist Church.[59] The black religion's tradition was expressed further in songs, testimonies, worship, and even in the protest movements. Protest against the political and social system of slavery gets much of its fuel from the religion of the slave. The black preacher was one of the most important and influential figures within the slave community. For it was he who exercised a powerful "political, social, moral and religious influence...on the slave."[60] Out of the great black religious tradition emerged such champions of abolition and freedom as Theodore Wright. Henry Highland Garnet and Daniel

A. Payne, to mention a few. The period under study indicates that the "black preacher was a molder of thought and character, and that he used the story of the

---

[59] Albert J. Raboteau. Slave Religion. (New York: Oxford University Press. 1980). pp. 214-215.

[60] Leon F. Litwack. North of Slavery, (Chicago, Illinois: The University of Chicago Press, 1970, pp. 191-192.

plight of ancient Israel as a divine model and precedent for emancipation from slavery." A number of anti-slavery organizations came into existence during the late 1820s and early 1830s which served as rallying points and power bulwarks against the social and political institution of slavery in the United States. In addition to the rapid upsurge of anti-slavery societies, there also emerged a significant number of prominent black preachers who added their voices to protest against slavery. From Boston came David Walker's famous Appeal that delivered a devastating blow to the slave system. In 1828 Walker appealed to slaves to "... rise up against the masters and protest against the intolerable conditions under which they were forced to live."[61]

It is against this cruel and atrocious form of slavery that was somehow allowed to coexist with and function under the disguise of Christianity that black religion registers an eternal protest. The following quote is an indication of the co-existence to which the present writer refers above: "I have seen a Christian professor, (one who confesses to being a Christian) after the communion, have four slaves tied together, and whipped raw, and then washed with beef Brinell."[62]

Black religion was a significant factor in preparing the slave for the revolts and protest movements whose ultimate objective was total freedom. The movements and societies organized to secure the freedom of the

---

[61] Carter G. Woodson. The Negro in our History, (Washington, D.C.: The Associated Publishing, Inc., 1922), pp. 72-73.

[62] John W. Blassingame, ed., Slave testimonies, (Baton Rouge, Louisiana: Louisiana State University Press, 1977), pp. 132- 140.

slaves eventually demanded the attention of those in the political and social arenas and played an invaluable role in the ultimate emancipation of the slaves. The attitude and revolutionary behavior of the Reverend David Walker expressed in the well-known David Walker's Appeal further testify to the impact of "black religion upon those whose life-work was given to the political emancipation of the slaves."[63]

Birney, Goodell, Wright, and May were strong and dedicated anti-slavery forces with which the pro-slavery elements had to reckon; however, there were untold numbers of blacks who were also deeply involved in the abolitionist movements, religious and political, to secure their own freedom. The vast majority of the black anti-slavery advocates sprang from religious roots. The name of Richard Allen. David Walker, Prince Hall, Absalom Jones, Frederick Douglass, and Nat Turner are somewhat synonymous with black religion and protest. Before the War for Independence, there are indications of black people's struggle for social and political freedom.[64] Black resistance to slavery was launched even at precarious risks to the very existence of those involved in the struggle. Black resistance, however, was not really on the same level as political insurrection, anarchy, or revolution; rather, black effort to actualize and bring to fruition a basic human goal and a divine decree, freedom was the ultimate goal. The courtroom testimony of an

---

[63] Peter K. Bergman. The Negro in America (New York: Harper and Row, 1969), pp.24-28

[64] John Hope Franklin. From Slavery to Freedom. (New York: Vintage Books, 1969), pp. 250-256.

anonymous black slave whose activities in the freedom struggle led to his arrest and trial suggests the level of commitment to freedom:

> "I have nothing more to offer than George Washington would have had to offer had he been taken by the British and put to trial by them. I have adventured my life in endeavoring to obtain the liberty of my Countrymen and their cause."

While political and social freedom was the ultimate goal, religion gave the struggle the added impetus needed to continue the drive toward the actualization of that goal. Vincent Harding points out in an article in August Meier and Elliott Rudwick's book, "The Making of Black America", Volume I, the significance of black religion in the freedom struggle of the black slaves and, also the initial appealing nature of Christianity to the slaves of the Roman Empire and to the black slaves in the Antebellum South. Harding is quite observant that religion in general and that black religion specifically have sustained, motivated, and provided the strength for survival during difficult situations.

He refers to the positions of Karl Marx, Benjamin Mays, and E. Franklin Frazier: Marx suggested that "Religion is the sign of the oppressed creature, the heart of the heartless world ... it is the opium of the people." Mays frequently saw the religion of the "Negro" as otherworldly and compensatory, while Frazier later defined black religion as a means of diverting attention from the horrors of day-to-day existence." It is rather tragic that such renowned scholars as Benjamin Mays and E. Franklin Frazier would define black religion as having such limited functions and other-worldly goals.[65]

There are others who define black religion as "essentially black protest" and as being minus the dualistic involvement that has as its focus the liberation of man in this world from the detestable and inhumane social, political, and economic conditions associated with slavery. However, in his The Black Experience in Religion, C. Eric Lincoln states "very clearly and authoritatively that for one to define black religion as simply a convert approach to political protest is not only an over-simplification of black religion. but is also a gross distortion."

There are strong suggestions that black religion during the period between 1800-1831 was deeply involved in social protest while refusing to lose sight of the spiritual, heavenly, otherworldly, and eschatological aspirations. Based upon these aspirations, the black liberation struggle of the slaves had an ever-present constant source of strength, black religion.[66] In the theologies of Nat Turner, David Walker, and even in the theological mind of Daniel Alexander Payne is evidence of the significant role of their religion in the struggle for freedom. Nat Turner was a viable exponent of a messianic concept and he felt that he had been divinely mobilized to lead the slaves out of bondage. David

---

[65] August Meier and Elliot Rudwick. The Making of Black America. (New York: Antheneum, 1969), pp. 155-156.

[66] Clement Eaton. The Freedom of the Thought in the Old South. (New York: Harper & Row Publishers, 1964). P. 90.

Walker's Appeal is saturated with the belief in a divine intervention into the deplorable social conditions of the black slaves. Daniel Alexander Payne, a foremost educator, preacher, and Anti-Slavery Advocate called for the immediate abolition of slavery. Payne's religious convictions were so strongly opposed to slavery that at several junctures in his experiences with the "Brutal" system he predicted that it would fall based on its inconsistency with the Will of God.[67] The Reverend David Walker, "called the John the Baptist of the Anti-Slavery Crusade," was a product of the emerging Anti-slavery sentiments among the predominantly black religious movements. Walker was a product of North Carolina but decided to migrate to Boston where he intensified his radical agitation which was designed to ultimately destroy the slave system. The large cadre of ministers who stood at the forefront of the Anti-slavery Crusades was not only deeply influenced by the Bible and religion, but also by the magnificent words of the Constitution and Declaration of Independence.[68]

During the eighteen-hundreds significant Abolitionist and Anti-slavery sentiments were operative within the confines of the religious community. While the black religious community was heavily committed to the immediate abolition of slavery, there were also concerted efforts on the part of predominantly white religious groups to rid the nation of the amazing social

---

[67] Henry J. Young. Major Black Religious Leaders. (Nashville, Tennessee: Abingdon Press, 1977), pp. 63-67.
[68] Larone Bennett Jr. Before the Mayflower, (Chicago, Illinois: Joan Publishing Company, Inc., 1969), pp. 132-134.

paradox of slavery: the Quakers stand at the forefront. The Reverend John Rankin, a Presbyterian, was a vocal white voice against slavery, and "Embree helped to build the Manumission Society of Tennessee."[69] Religion in general and the religion of the slave have had a tremendous impact on the formation of his desire for freedom and have been a significant force in mobilizing him to achieve total freedom.

In actuality, the freedom struggle of the black slave began even before they were brought to the shores of the New World. The slave's protest for freedom began immediately following his capture in Africa and the preparation for transportation to the American shores. There were attempts to escape their captors while the

en route to the barracoons and even after being loaded onto the ships, freedom was an inevitable yearning of black slaves. It has been suggested that one reason for the struggle for liberation was due to a belief among the slaves that their white captors would eventually eat them, and "Rather than becoming a delicacy for a foreign cannibalistic, vicious white slave master, they chose death by leaping overboard ships, and even resorting to other means of suicide."

The Black Church and Black religious organizations historically have been at the forefront of the liberation struggle and have, through a number of efforts, continued to register their unrest as long as slavery continued to reveal its ugly face in America. This is,

---

[69] Louis Filler, The Crusade Against Slavery. (New York: Harper and Brothers Publishers, 1960), pp. 15-17.

of course, contrary to a number of assertions made by white sociologists, and by a few black sociologists and theologians. The position has been that black religion has been passive, docile, uninvolved, and even disinterested in the earthly condition of the slaves. It has been posited by Benjamin Mays that black religion was primarily involved with otherworldly concerns rather than the existential harrows of slavery. While this was perhaps true among some circles of slaves and slave preachers, it is not a totally accurate assessment of the slave community at large. Historically black religion has been aware of and opposed to the obvious inconsistency that existed between what white Christianity said and what its adherents did.

The eventual separation of the black communicants from the white Methodist church is an eternal reminder of blacks' recognition of such inconsistencies in the white form of the Christian religion. When Richard Allen and Absalom Jones became unwilling to submit to second-class status in the white-dominated St. George's Methodist Church in Philadelphia, they set in motion a church-sponsored protest movement against slavery in the church.[70] Slavery in the church was relatively microscopic of a much larger societal phenomenon whose ripple effect was felt over a large segment of the United States.

The thirst for freedom was inherent within the slave community and the fires of freedom were fueled not

---

[70] Carletone. Black Freedom. (London, England: The McMillan Company, 1970), pp. 133-134.

only by the obvious moral evils associated with the slave system, but by the magnificent words of the Declaration of Independence, the Constitution of the United States, and the news of the freedom struggle in the Caribbean areas.[71] The Negro slave was an unmanageable piece of the property despite his status as a dehumanized chattel slave. He was as uncomfortable as a caged bird and never fully allowed himself to be at ease under a system that rendered him only a means to an end rather than an end within himself. From the very inception of the black church in the United States, there was the ultimate goal of total freedom of the slave. Slavery was never fully accepted by the slave as being in his best interest nor as a God-ordained institution whose benevolent aim was to civilize the heathens, introduce them to Christianity and ultimately save their souls in heaven by and by.

Therefore, the pie-in-sky mentality was developed in the minds of the slave master and was perpetrated upon some slaves who had negated all hope of ever transcending their slave status on earth. Thus, for the slave who saw freedom in this life as an unachievable reality, he shifted his attention from a perceived earthly impossibility to an otherworldly, transcendent possibility. One cannot deny that spiritualization of the summum bonum did occur among some slaves. But docility and the acceptance of and satisfaction with slave status was always an unrealized goal of the slave master. The slave continued to be an unmanageable and a "...

---

[71] Clement Eaton. The Freedom Thought in the Old South. (New York: Harper & Row Publishing, Inc., 1964), pp. 90-91.

troublesome piece of property,"[72] who would settle for nothing less than total freedom. Total freedom for the slave meant not just total religious freedom but political, social, and economic freedom as well. The white slave masters' attempt to use his brand of the Christian religion to render the slave docile, and manageable and to make him a more productive servant failed. But not before he went to great lengths to expose his slave to the Christian religion. It is true that the first form of education to which the stave was exposed was religious education that took place within the confines of the benevolent master's home, or at his house of worship.

Black slaves displayed an exceptionally deep desire to raise themselves to literate status.[73] The slave understood quite early the connection between knowledge and power, or the power associated with knowledge. Therefore, when blacks applied themselves to learning, there was always the covert motivation that to learn was tantamount to preparing oneself for the ultimate liberation smuggle. It is evident that when blacks learned to read the Bible they were immediately exposed to and made aware of certain themes that run through the Bible: liberation, freedom, justice, and the equal status of all Christians. The slave was always appalled at the master's attempts to force Christianity to accommodate his own political and selfish ends. An eternal reminder of such attempts (sometimes

---

[72] Kenneth M. Stampp. <u>The Peculiar Institution</u>. (New York: Alfred A. Knopf, 1969), pp. 128-129.

[73] Leslie Howard Owens. <u>The Species of Property</u>. (New York: Oxford University Press, 1976), pp. 163.

successful) was the retention of the services of the white preacher who almost always tended to support the status quo of white folks' Christianity. However, it was soon detected by uneducated (as seen by white folks) slaves, the incompatibility of Christianity and Slavery. Quite early did the slave refuse the otherworldly focus suggested to him by the slave master's preacher? The typical sermons preached by the white preacher, and to which Blacks were subjected, are reflected below: "You slaves will go to heaven if you are good, but don't ever think that you will be close to your mistress and master, No! No! There will be a wall between you: but there will be holes in it that will permit you to look out and see your mistress when she passes by. If you want to sit behind this wall, you must do the language of the text. Obey your masters."

It is this kind of theology to which the slave was subjected and was presented the awesome challenge of deciphering the difference between authentic Christianity and the blatant pragmatic and arbitrary applications made by the white preacher. It was inconceivable, first of all, that a slave would want to be in the same heaven with his former master, not to mention peering at him through a hole in the wall. Another famous sermon that most slaves heard from the White slave master's preacher was: "Serve your master. Don't steal your master's turkey. Don't steal your master's chickens. Don't steal your master's hawgs.

Don't steal your master's meat ..."[74] It was to this level of white folk's prostitution of Christianity that gave rise to black religion in the United States. White black religion had its origin as an invisible institution. the covert and perpetual motivation and the ultimate goal was total liberation.

White the white-oriented brands of the Christian religion preoccupied themselves with such concerns as the establishment of Christianity in Colonial America, a complete Christian commonwealth, and the Christian conquest of the world, the black slave was primarily concerned with the conquest of slavery and the establishment of total freedom. Therefore, a religious attempt to domesticate, civilize and make the slave more docile and economically productive held a seed of destruction for the slave institution in America. What the slave master did not fully understand was that no person, slave or free, can have a genuine, authentic encounter with Jesus Christ and Christianity and remain a genuine, authentic supporter of slavery in any form. The slave was able to conceptualize, internalize, analyze and revitalize the reality of authentic Christianity. Therefore, he led the struggle to actualize what is a basic tenet of the Christian religion that whites had either deliberately or ignorantly overlooked. In light of this theological violence done to the biblical text in an effort to promote second-class people on earth and inferior Christians in heaven, the slaves along with the

---

[74] Arkansas Rawick. God Struck Me Dead. (Philadelphia, Pennsylvania: Pilgrim Press, 1969), pp. 134-135.

slave preachers carved out of their existential dilemma. based upon the Bible. a strategy for survival in a hostile environment and a means for achieving total freedom.

The freedom struggle, while born before the slaves left the shores of Africa, developed into a viable movement in America with the rise of the "invisible" church. The development of the "invisible" church was itself a protest movement against the white man's religion. It developed as a result of the irrelevancies of the white preacher's sermons to the needs of the black people. For the slave to hear sermons that were relevant and made sense to him, he had to resort to the black slave preacher who also lived the experiences of his parishioners. The testimony of a slave, Lucretia Alexander is quite typical of what black people did when they could no longer tolerate the one-sided sermons of the white preacher. Those feelings of black folks are expressed in the following: "Do whatever your master tells you to do. The same old thing all the time. My father would have church in dwelling houses and they had to whisper ... sometimes they would have church at his house. when they wanted a real meetin' with some real preachin'."[75] This is the nature of complaints registered by blacks who were a part of white-run churches during slavery, and thus led to the eventual separation of blacks and whites as seen in the Richard Allen and Absalom Jones church-related controversy in 1787. While Allen and Jones were freedmen, they were continually

---

[75] Albert J. Raboteau <u>Slave Region</u>. (New York: Oxford University Press, 1978), pp. 214-215.

subjected to second-class status even in worship and at the altar rail during holy Communion. Incidents of these magnitudes would eventually prove unbearable for black Christians in white-run churches, thus giving rise to the invisible. visible, and ultimately the establishment of the independent black church in the United States. From the black pulpit would emanate the clarion call for the total liberation of the slaves.[76]

Within the slave quarters there developed a mentality, an aspiration, and a movement within eyesight of the "Big House" that defined the social, religious, and political norms of the late seventeen and early eighteen-hundreds. The slaves' religious understanding and conviction of the justice and mercy of the God of Moses, Joshua, Daniel, and Jesus Christ were powerfully motivating for the task that lay ahead. Within the slave community there developed both formal and informal leadership. However, the most powerful form of leadership rested in the black preacher. It was he who, in most situations, was better educated and had made some confession of being divinely called to preach. Often times the black slave preacher would report having seen visions, or some extraordinary telepathy that further authenticated his call. A noted sociologist, W.E.B, DuBois, observed several characteristics of the black slave religion, one of which was the preacher. DuBois was quite perceptive in his observations that "the preacher is the most unique personality developed by the Negro

---

[76] Leon F. Litwack <u>North of Slavery</u>, (Chicago Illinois: The University of Chicago Press, 1970), p. 191.

on American soil.'" The preacher was "...a leader, a politician, an orator, a 'boss', an intriguer, an idealist..."[77] DuBois has touched the core of the role and function of the black preacher in the slave community. The black preacher was not necessarily a revolutionary agitator, however, if the situation necessitated such action, there were the biblical precedents of Moses and Joshua as points of reference. As a rule of thumb, the black preacher was always seen as a possible revolutionary and an agitator by the slave system that was to be kept under surveillance; for his political tendencies were always unpredictable.[78]

The Black Church's origin is due partly to a massive protest movement formed in the white church and ultimately led to blacks being expelled from white churches. The expulsion itself reflects the development of a church within a church. There was within the leading religious' denominations of the slave era a segment of the congregation whose religious and theological beliefs differed one from the other. It was out of such religious atmospheres that emerged the feelings of the need for physical separation of blacks from the predominantly white congregations.

Blacks were not totally adverse to the move and showed little resistance because they had become disturbed with the second-class status placed upon them in worship and as fellow humans, for the hostilities

---

[77] W.E.B DuBois. Souls of the Black Folk. (New York: Fawcett Publications, Inc., 1961), p. 141.
[78] Eugene D. Genovese. Roll Jordan Roll. (New York: Pantheon Books, 1974), pp. 258-259.

of whites tended to force blacks in the direction of separation. However, for blacks, the move was both a positive and welcoming gesture in the sense that it brought blacks a few steps closer to the reality of independence and an opportunity to establish their own church.

The rise of the independent or separate Black Church was not necessarily a spontaneous reality. The long road to the establishment of the independent Black Church took on many forms and shapes given the nature and opportunity of the situation. Perhaps the first effort towards independence in religious worship and to establish their own church was what E. Franklin Frazier called the "Invisible Institution." From the first encounter of whites and black Africans, there was evidence of the Africans being deeply religious people. Melville J. Herskovits is quite alert to detect the slaves' retention of an aspect of his religion as it relates to baptism by total immersion. He advances the idea that the large attraction of the slave to the Baptist religion was due largely to the close similarity to the "...Water Cults of Nigeria and Dahomey." The exact time and place of origin of the "Invisible Institution" is quite difficult to establish. However, the extended freedom enjoyed by the slave in the slave quarters on the plantation perhaps gave rise to the invisible church. While the location of the slave quarters was in relatively close proximity to the "Big House", they were far enough away to allow for some autonomy and a time for a retreat from the watchful eyes of the master and overseer. The slave quarters provided a place for social functions and relaxation at the close of the workday.

The time left alone in the slave quarters gave the slave ample time to reflect, think, process and develop what is seen as the invisible church. The church was invisible in the sense that it somehow escaped, to some significance, the detection, watchful eye, and control of the slave master. At times this lack of interference by the master[79] ... gave bondsmen a free hand[80], in mapping strategy for not only their religious needs but for planning their political future. It was in the slave quarters that slaves learned the advantages of corporate solidarity and of combining resources for the good of the community. They learned and practiced joint ventures from collecting firewood to sharing the bounty of a successful hunt. The slaves worked together, cooked together, and lived together in the slave quarters. It was in the slave quarters and from the slave experience that the slave learned a lesson that would prove invaluable to his future efforts to gain his freedom. The existence of the invisible church, while microscopic, was by no means an insignificant milestone on the road to black freedom. Prior to the official separation of blacks from the white churches, bondsmen and freemen worshipped together in the same physical structure. This system accomplished two objectives one was to keep a watchful eye on the slave during his communication with God,

---

[79] James Curtis Ballagh. A History of Slavery in Virginia. (Baltimore, Maryland: Johns Hopkins University Press, 1902), p. 107.

[80] Leslie Howard Owens. The Species of Property, (New York: Oxford University Press, 1976), p. 153-154.

and two was to satisfy his role to provide Christian education for his slaves. The slave master held the slave in suspicion during worship, for there was the strong belief that the slave was praying down damnation on his master. The report of an ex-slave is indicative of the master's perception of the slave's religious worship meetings: "Most of them thought that when Colored people were praying it was against them. For when they would catch them praying for God to lift things out of their way and the white folks would lift them (the slaves)." However, there were times when whites would join in with blacks in worship, thus with the joining of whites in worship with the blacks there existed in the white man's mind a sense of control over blacks. But even within those joint worship experiences, blacks would resort to the codified Language that was understood only by another black.

It is noteworthy that blacks constituted a significant percentage of the two major denominations, the Methodist and Baptist Churches. As early as 1790, the Methodist Church in Virginia consisted of one-fifth of blacks, and it is believed that the percentage of the Baptist Church was even higher.[81]

The second-class status imposed upon blacks by the leading religious denominations coupled with the irrelevancy of the worship experiences contributed to the use of the invisible church that ultimately led to the free independent black churches during the

---

[81] Albert J. Raboteau. <u>Slave Religion</u>. (New York: Oxford University Press, 1978), p. 214.

eighteenth and nineteenth Centuries. It was during the invisible church setting that the idea of freedom was conceptualized, nurtured, and eventually actualized in the attempts of revolutionaries to rid the nation of slavery in the same sense as was done by George Washington and Patrick Henry. There were such men as those in New York City in 1712, or South Carolina in 1739, a Gabriel Prosser in Richmond, Virginia in 1800, or a Denmark Vesey in Charleston, South Carolina in 1822, to such a person as David Walker in 1829 and, a Nat Turner in 1831 whose total aim was to rid the nation of slavery. For the most part, the leaders of these revolutionary movements had significant religious connections, either with the visible church as did David Walker or with the invisible church as did Nat Turner.

The slaves who sat in white-run churches detected the inconsistency between slavery and white Christianity. The obvious contradictions in white Christianity led the slaves to develop a theology of life and struggle whose meaning was ably propagated by the black preacher in the slave community. The brand of Christianity fashioned in the slave quarters reflected a combination of traditional Christianity where mutual love, respect, and togetherness were emphasized and; at the same time, emphasized Christianity as a viable force against the dehumanizing efforts of white Christians. Eugene Genovese is quite observant and takes the position that slave religion did not emerge as a result of a failed slave revolt nor was the failure of slave revolts due to black Christianity.[82] The Christianity that developed within the "Invisible Church" was a solid, viable Christianity that not only had at the core of the movement the consideration and purpose of the eventual liberation of the slave but their subsequent survival as well. Through a careful analysis of the reality of the slave master's commitment to maintaining slavery at any cost, the planners of revolutionary actions considered that an out-thought of a premature move that held the possibility of annihilation that would serve no positive end, while a carefully planned and conscious effort would prove beneficial in the long run. Nonetheless, the slaves never abandoned their expectation of eventual freedom. neither did they expect freedom to come as a solely cosmic eschatological event. rather, they saw themselves as cooperating with God in the divine scheme of deliverance.

Therefore, the slave's religion became one of the most potent weapons for change of their social, economic, and political status in a hostile environment. The slave's religious orientation refused to dichotomize the this-worldly and the other-worldly, rather they saw religion as having significant implications for both worlds. Religion for the slave meant freedom, a freedom that is not conferred by nor taken away by man or the State; rather it was God-given and was to be enjoyed by all men equally. Therefore, the theological positions of slave inferiority and the concept of a divinely-ordained

---

[82] Eugene D. Genovese. From Rebellion to Revolution. (Baton Rouge: Louisiana State University Press, 1979), pp. 44-45.

subjection to slavery, whether emanating from the slave master or from the Bishop of London, had very little effect on slave submission to the slave system. The slaves continued to understand that God was involved with them in a divine-human enterprise in their struggle for freedom.

Within the slave community, there was a blending together of biblical themes that had at their core, liberation. A slave's testimony advances the idea of the God-man struggle for freedom:

> "He have been wid us, Jesus, He still wid us, Jesus, He still wid us, Jesus. He will be wid us, Jesus, Be wid us to the end."[83] . . . or I been preaching the Gospel and farmin' since slavery time ... When I starts preachin' I couldn't read or write and lead to preach what massa told me ...but I knowed there's something better for them, but tell them but on the sly. That I done lots. I tell lem iffen they keeps prayin' the Lord will set lem free.'"[84]

The fact that the slave recognized that "Jesus is wid us" implies a corporate effort on the part of God and man in the freedom struggle. How was it possible for the God of the white slave master to be the same God as the black slaves? This is not an easy question to answer. However, there is very little doubt that the religion of

---

[83] Ibid., pp. 44-45
[84] Albert J. Raboteau. <u>Slave Religion</u> (New York: Oxford University Press, 1978), p. 214.

blacks from their capture in Africa to the present have been predisposed to the beliefs held sacred by the Judeo-Christian religion. One possible explanation is that while blacks did not reject totally the white man's interpretation of the Judeo-Christian religion, they exercised a degree of eclecticism in deciding which of the tenets offered them that they would accept and adopt as their guide for living. It is this degree of eclecticism that gave rise to the "Invisible Church" and gave us the separate, independent Black Church."[85]

The Black Church was born out of protest and she has never fully forgotten the nature of her origin and mission. In the slave quarters, away from the watchful eye of the slave master, she chartered a course that would lead to eventual liberation. While there were, unquestionably, large numbers of persons instrumental in making freedom a reality, the black slave preacher stood as an unmovable symbol of God's presence in the struggle. The nature of the black preacher's sermon u as a Revolutionary fervor. Black people needed their preacher and they relied on his divine insights and natural wit to steer them clear of the slave masters' obstacles and to guide them safely to better days ahead.

---

[85] Gayraud S. Wilmore. Black Religion and Black Radicalism. (Garden City: Doubleday and Company, Inc., 1972), p. 2.

CHAPTER V

NATHANIEL PAUL'S STRUGGLES FOR THE ABOLITION OF SLAVERY

Before there was a Declaration of Independence, a Constitution of the United States of America, an Anti-slavery movement, an Abolitionist organization, a Civil Rights movement, a Malcolm X, and a Martin Luther King. Jr., there was a freedom struggle among enslaved people to win their freedom. The struggle for freedom, as it involves Afro-Americans, began on the shores of Africa, continued during the sojourn in the barracoons, the "Middle Passage" and, is alive even today among freedom-hungry' and freedom-loving peoples of the world. Freedom is an insatiable aspiration of man. Freedom is an inherent desire of most people. Freedom is more a state of being or quality of condition than it is a status conferred by the state. Freedom is not so much a human trait as it is a state of being, given by a power that transcends all human powers, authorities, and systems. Freedom is a quality of life bequeathed to human creation by the Creator of the universe and of humankind.

Freedom from slave catchers (black and white) on the coast of West Africa, liberation from involuntary bondage in the United States, and, the opportunity to live out one's divine destiny was eternal aspiration of most slaves. Political, social, and economic freedom was an undiminished desire that was "insatiable by the existential situation of slavery." Accordingly, a former slave expressed the typical and eternal longing held by the majority of slaves from the capturing of the first slave until the last one is freed: "Freedom indeed, free from death, free from hell, free from work, free from white folks, free from everything." Freedom was an ever-present goal of the slave, a daily preoccupation and a future reality to be achieved by u whatever means necessary, even if the quest for that freedom involved the loss of personal life.

Freedom was priceless, God-ordained; and, therefore, no person had the right to enslave another. The core of the concept of freedom that pervaded the period, 1755-1800, is based upon the slaves' understanding of" natural laws and the natural rights of man. The purpose of this chapter is to cite and examine various concepts of freedom as were espoused during the last four decades of the Eighteenth-century in the United States of America, which was during the height of chattel slavery. There arose in the mid-1700s two black churchmen, Nathaniel Paul and Richard Allen, who committed themselves to the freedom struggle of the slave. Nathaniel Paul was born in 1755, as best as can be authenticated, in Albany, New York, where he served as pastor of the African Baptist church. Paul eventually terminated his pastoral responsibilities at the African Baptist church and gave his life, in later years, to antislavery activities. In 1827, twelve years before his death in 1839, Paul gave his most famous address during the celebration of the abolition of slavery in the State of New York." The Address was entitled, "An address delivered on the celebration of the Abolition of Slavery in the State of New York."[86] Thus Paul became one of the early pioneers of the antislavery effort in the United States. His concept of freedom was developed and was being acted out in history before there Williams L. Harrison, Charles Sumner, and Wendel Phillips were on the scene. Paul's concept of freedom was born, nurtured, and developed in light of the existential situation of slavery. Nathaniel Paul's concept of freedom was deeply rooted In his theology and in his understanding of the will of God.

THEOLOGICAL ORIENTATIONS AGAINST SLAVERY

Theologically, Paul encountered serious personal difficulty in what he saw as an inconsistency between the reality of God and the existence of slavery. He understood God as being both immanent in His world and at the same time transcendent above His world.

---

[86] Henry Clay Bruce. The New Man: Twenty-Nine Years as a Free Man. (York, Pa: Anstadt Press, 1895), p. 73.

What Paul believed, essentially, was that God is active in His world in the historical affairs of His creation, but that He is not confined or limited to His world. This dual and universal location of God made Him an unrevealed mystery that was not fully comprehensible to the human mind. However, Paul understood this as a reality of God in man when man's efforts were directed toward liberation from the institution of slavery.

Paul's understanding of the sovereignty of God allowed him to become pessimistic at times, and he even questioned the acts of God.[87] Paul, at an earlier stage in his development. thought that the death of the slaves at sea would have been better than slavery in America. Paul's concept of freedom emerged as a result of his sense of frequent engagements in dialogue with God. At one point in Paul's agony over slaves and their inconsistency with divine justice, he raised the philosophical and existential question: "Why did the waters of the ocean sustain the. Cruel misery of human bondage ...?" For him, the slave experienced "the most abject state of degraded misery." Nathaniel Paul's conception of freedom was deeply rooted in the social phenomena of the eighteenth and nineteenth centuries of American life: half slave and half free. Out of the inconsistency of the social phenomena, Paul arrived at what he understood as sin, Sin, for Paul, was disobedience to God's will for freedom of all people. The slave system was a constant

---

[87] Carter G. Woodson. The Mind of the Negro as is Reflected in Letters During the Crisis: 1800-1860. (New York: Negro University Press, 1969), p. 163.

symbol of that sin of disobedience to God's will of freedom. He further protested the situation of the slave by raising the question of whether God and slavery are, in fact, contradictions. However, the question was more rhetorical than theological inquiry. for Paul had already formulated the concept of the inconsistency between slavery and God. The supreme question to which lie wanted a definitive answer was, "Why are black people living in servitude?" Paul could have easily answered that question without involving God. and he had done so already, by examining the socio-cultural milieu and the political climate of his own time.[88] However, it seems much easier for Paul to raise these questions to God directly rather than seek to dialogue with the slave master. In a typical dialogue with God, Paul raises these questions:

> "And, Oh thou immaculate God, be not angry with us while we come into this thy sanctuary, and make the bold inquiry in this thy holy temple, why it was that thou didst look on with calm indifference of an unconcerned spectator when thy holy law was violated, thy divine authority despised and a portion of thine on n creatures reduced to a state of here vassalage and misery?"

The divine-human dialogue between God and Nathaniel Paul reveals Paul's dilemma that was created by the historical reality of slavery. Paul's appeal to

---

[88] Henry J. Young. <u>Major Black Religious Leaders</u>, (Nashville, Tennessee: Abingdon Press, 1977), p. 21.

the God of history, and of Israel, provided for him some degree of assurance that God's deliverance was imminent.

Herein lies the sum total of Paul's concept of freedom. Paul espoused the position that a sovereign, righteous God would bring about freedom for all of His creation. The abolition of slaves in the State of New York in 1827 was a further indication of God's activity on the part of freedom. Paul hailed that historical reality as a sign of God's liberating power. Paul did not minimize the effective potency of a divine-human enterprise. Neither was his reliance upon God for total liberation an attempt to make human liberation solely a divine responsibility, or only another worldly possibility.[89] However, Paul was able to focus beyond the tragedy of the moment and see coming out of slavery, or evil, something good. "It was the gracious ordinance of providence, both in the natural and moral world that good should arise out of evil."

Paul's address on July 5, 1827, is a most pointed attack on the system of slavery and is a vivid testimony to his vociferous effort to eradicate the nation of moral evil. Paul's struggle with the question of the inconsistency between the reality of slavery and the Inherent goodness of God provided a basis for Walker's condemnation of slavery. "Tell me, ye mighty waters, why did ye sustain the ponderous load of misery?" comes close to pessimism on the one hand, but sounds like a rhetorical question on the other hand. But

---

[89] Carter G. Woodson. Negro Orators and Their Orations. (Washington. D.C.: Associated Publishers. 1925), p. 69.

Paul answers his own question: "Be still, and know that I am God!'" Paul's resolution to his dilemma was reached by appealing to the intrinsic goodness of God, and his confession that God alone can bring good out of evil. Paul seems to question the act of God, but he always concludes his pessimistic tirades with a diminished position that God is in control of history and of man. With that resolution, he and Walker share a common theology as to God's plan in the out of some of the slavery. In Paul's July 5, 1 827 address is stated "... that our (God 1s a God of justice, and no respected of persons",[90] which is a similar position taken by Walker whose religious beliefs led him to confess that

> "I cannot but bless God for the glorious anticipation of a not very distant period, when those things which most help to degrade us will be no more ... among the sons of Africa."

Nathaniel Paul's concept of freedom closely parallels that of David Walker, who held to both God's imminence and His transcendence. which provided for Walker a basis for God's active involvement in the world. Just as Paul could categorically assert that God did not create an inferior nor a superior creature in his human creation and, therefore in the eyes of God all persons are of equal significance. Thus Paul's eschatology is evident here in the sense that man, even the slave, is moving

---

[90] Nathaniel Paul. An Address, Deliverved on the Celebration of the Abolition oi Slavery in the State of New York. (Albany. New York: John B. Van Steenbergh, 1827). pp. 8-9.

toward God's ultimate goal and purpose for him. The consistency between Paul's and Walker's positions on God's involvement on the part of the slave is seen in Walker's <u>Appeal</u>," ... they are so happy to keep in ignorance and degradation ... the labor of the slave, they forget that God rules in the armies of heaven ...having his ears continually open to the cries. tears and groans of his oppressed people ...will one day appear fully on behalf of the oppressed."[91] Nathaniel Paul, whose speech was delivered on the anniversary of the abolition of slavery in New York, because of the similar contents of his message to that of David Walker, influences Walker's concept of freedom. While both Paul and Walker felt that the hand of God was involved in slavery, they did not see that as an excuse for human non-involvement, for out of the cruel system of slavery, they envisioned good will come.

Paul's words sound similar to Walker's during the abolitionist speech, "It was the gracious ordinance of providence, both in the natural and moral world that good should often arise out of evil. Paul's position finds some support in Walker's position on the question, "Will He let the oppressors rest comfortably and happy always? Will He hot cause the very children of the oppressors to rise up against them, and off times put them to death? "God works in many ways His wonders to perform." The contents of the <u>Appeal</u>, coupled with Walker's speeches support the position that Nathaniel Paul had an effect on the formation of Walker's thoughts. Their lives overlapped, they both lived in the Eastern

---

[91] "<u>Freedom's Journal</u>". November 2. 1827. Vol, No. 34.

part of the United States, and both of them were staunch enemies of the slave system. Their parallel views that God was involved with a man in the eradication of slavery place both of them among those who viewed freedom as a divine-human enterprise.[92] For Nathaniel David, this meant that the forces of heaven and earth are partners in liberation.

Richard Allen

David Walker was influenced by a number of abolitionists, some of whom were his contemporaries and others who preceded him in life and overlapped him: Nathaniel Paul and Richard Allen. The person who had the most profound effect on the life of Walker was the Reverend Richard Allen. Richard Allen was born on February 14, 1760, in Philadelphia, Pennsylvania. Allen was a part of the slave holdings of Benjamin in Chew. Allen spent much of his life as a slave in the State of Delaware, near Dover. The 1760s were severe economic times and necessitated the sale of slave property by Mr. Chew. The Allen family was one of the families sold. The sale of the Allen's was not an unusual event because, in the eyes of slaveholders, slavery was a domestic event that involved the transfer of property for economic gain. Therefore, in the Allen family, the father. mother and four children simply joined, by economic design, the "innumerable caravan" of homeless chattel sold to ensure the perpetual wealth of Benjamin Chew.

---

[92] William Laren Katz. (New York: Arno Press and The New York Times, 1827), pp. 15.

The chronology of Richard Allen's life immediately presents a degree of difficulty. Being a chattel slave did not mandate meticulous statistical data on the welfare of a slave. However, as best as can be ascertained, Allen returned to Philadelphia, Pennsylvania around 1786 and established there as a permanent resident. Philadelphia would eventually become the city in which Allen was to live and make lasting contributions to the Protestant religion in America. Allen had originally embraced the Methodist religious faith at a young age while yet in the State of Delaware. It is believed that the sale of a younger brother and sister, coupled with the death of his parents led him to seek strength in the Methodist religion. Allen was initiated on the Stokeley's farm during one of the visits of the circuit rider revivals. The tenets of Methodism that influenced Allen were the emphasis on personal conversion and individual responsibility. The remainder of Allen's life was to reflect these tenets of his religious faith. As an adherent of the Methodist faith, he fell into, what he perceived as its stance against slavery. Methodism, since John Wesley, had taken a position against slavery and had set forth in the Methodist Discipline an attack on the institution of slavery.[93]

The life of Richard Allen is synonymous with protest. It is unthinkable, given the history of his later life, that Allen was a docile slave who never spoke out against the horrors of slavery. Allen's protest efforts reached a new

---

[93] Carol V. R. George. Segregated Sabbaths: Richard Allen and the Emergence of Independent Black Churches. (New York: Oxford University Press, 1973), pp. 21-23.

height in November 1787 during a worship service at St. George Methodist Episcopal Church in Philadelphia, Pennsylvania when Allen and Absalom Jones were ejected from the church. Blacks had been formerly allowed to worship with whites on the main floor, but the numbers of blacks continued to increase, thus the policy of relegating blacks to the galleries was initiated. But rather than sitting in the rear of the gallery, Absalom Jones and Richard Allen gravitated to the front. While on their knees during the period of prayer, Allen later stated. "We had not been long upon our knees before I heard considerable scuffling and low talking. I raised my head up and saw one of the trustees ... having hold of the Reverend Absalom Jones, pulling him up off of his knees, and saying, 'You must get up - you must not kneel here."

The incident in St. George Methodist Episcopal Church is the occasion that catapulted Allen into the limelight of history. During the incident, both Allen and Jones, along with other blacks, walked out of the church together. This incident provided the blacks with ... fresh vigor to get a house erected to worship God in. Jones confesses that this exit by Allen and his companions was a prophetic protest against segregated worship.[94] Allen and Jones' faith in God and their commitment to freedom and equality formed, for them, the basis and point of departure for liberation." It was this basic understanding of God and zeal for freedom in Richard Allen that influenced David Walker. To get a deeper sense of and feel for the image

---

[94] Leon F. Litwack. North of Slavery. (Chicago. Illinois: University of Chicago Press, 1970). p. 191.

of Allen in the mind of Walker. one needs to take note of the reference to Allen in Article IV of Walker's Appeal,[95] "I shall give on an extract from the letter of that truly Reverend Divine of Philadelphia ...' Like Allen, Walker detested the idea of the colonizing of Africans iii Liberia. Allen's anti-colonization stance and his protest against slavery were crucial to the formation of Walker's concept of freedom. Allen took a firm position against slavery and allowed a public forum to be held at historic Bethel Church in Philadelphia, Pennsylvania where hundreds of protesters gathered to oppose the colonization movement. Allen's article in Freedom's Journal, November 2, 1827, is the statement that most profoundly affected Walker's concept of freedom, "This land which we have watered with our tears and our blood, is now our mother country, and we are well satisfied to stay where wisdom abounds and the gospel is free." Allen's firm position against sending blacks to Africa, coupled with his zeal for freedom of the slaves found support in David Walker's struggle for freedom of the slave.

Like Allen, Walker believed that God's plan was also his plan and that God was with him and the slave community in the liberation struggle. Like Allen, Walker continually reveals a sense of interdependence, interconnectedness, and interrelatedness between God and man.[96] This firm conviction moved Allen to oppose slavery, speak out against injustice, and become one of

---

[95] James Cone. God of the Oppressed. (New York: The Seabury Press, 1975), pp. 12-15.
[96] "Freedoms Journal", November 2, 1827. Vol I, No.34.

the true champions of social justice during nineteenth-century America. Richard Allen was instrumental in not only the breaking of blacks from the white church but was also a leader of great influence in the Free African Society and served, along with Absalom Jones, as one of its early leaders. One of Allen's preoccupations was the separation of blacks from the white church.

The zeal for separation, coupled with a quest for Negro identity, led to aggressive efforts to purchase property and build a church building to become dominated and led by blacks. Allen conceived the black church as a power base, and his idea has led to the reality that the only institution owned, led, and controlled by blacks in the United States is the Black Church.

For Allen to be a companion of Jones or vice versa, is an indication of the detestable conditions of slavery, and an example that equality could only become a reality in a separated state. Allen championed the cause of religious separation as did David Walker championed the cause of freedom and the annihilation of the slave system. David Walker literally urged slaves to fight for their freedom.

The religious and social freedom inherent within the idea of Allen as he sought physical, religious, and political separation is the aspect of Allen's commitment to freedom that registered in the formation of Walker's concept of freedom. Walker idolized Allen as a god, "that truly Reverend Divine", and continued to use the Allen approach in his writings and speeches.

Walker follows in the pioneering spirit of Allen as is reflected in a speech given during a meeting of the Freedom's Journal organization held in Boston,

Massachusetts, on March 26, 1828, in which he stated that "the very derision, violence, and oppression, with which we as a part of the community are treated by a benevolent and Christian people, ought to stimulate us to the greatest exertion for the acquirement both of literature and property, for although we may complain of the almost in-hospitability with which we are treated; yet if we continue to slumber on and take our ease, our wheel of reformation will progress but slowly."[97]

As Allen saw the wheels of black progress as turning too slowly while blacks remained in predominately white churches, Walker felt that if blacks ", continued to slumber and take our ease ...the wheels will progress but slowly. Immediate action, abrupt change, and personal involvement were the keys to speed up progress for the black race, were the vocal positions of both Allen and Walker." To read Walker's speech given before the General Colored Association of Boston, on December 19, 1828, is to hear the resounding echoes of Allen, in essence: "Mr. President, the primary object of this institution is to unite the colored population."[98] Allen's concept of freedom had a lasting impact on the formation of Walker's concept of freedom which is seen at various significant junctures of Walker's Appeal.

Allen's rejection of white domination in the religious arena is reflected by Walker's rejection of white domination in the political arena. As Allen's struggle

---

[97] Carol V. R. George. Segregated Sabbaths: Richard Allen and the Emergence of the Independent Black Churches. (New York: Oxford University Press, 1973), pp. 21-23.

[98] "Freedom's Journal", April 25, 1828, Vol. 2, No. 5. p. 398.

for freedom of the slave took him deeply into political and social arenas, Walker's struggle also took him deeply into religious and political arenas. Allen made a break with the organized St. George's Church in order to establish the credibility of the black community thus providing a means of black domination and direction. Like Allen, Walker's Appeal challenged the legitimacy of white rule in all aspects of black life. Both leaders were able to see the consistency of attitudes and practices in the religious and political realm of existence[99] As Vincent Harding points out, "... while political leaders of 1787 did not make the issue of black freedom a paid of the revolutionary rhetoric, neither did their Christianity extends to the auction block."[100]

Inherent within the revolutionary psyche was total freedom. Freedom was the language of the streets, the shops. the home, and of the political arena. It is safe to posit that since the arrival of the first European on the shores of this "New World", freedom was the primary preoccupation and an insatiable desire. The de- sire for freedom did not simply involve white Europeans; Africans were also a part of that desire. Nathaniel Paul and Richard Allen laid some fertile grounds tor David Walker, whose appeal was to echo, in years to come, the same zeal for freedom.

---

[99] "Freedom's Journal, December 19, 1828. Vol. II, p. 298.
[100] Vinccnt Harding. There is A River. (New York: Harcourt Brace and Jovanovich, 1981), pp. 44-45.

CHAPTER VI
DAVID WALKER'S CONCEPT OF FREEDOM

Following the historic and decisive military march of Union General, General Sherman, from Atlanta, Georgia to Savannah, Georgia in 1865, one of the first orders of business was to convene a meeting between himself and the black leaders of Savannah. General Sherman and Edwin M. Stanton, Secretary of War, convened the meeting. The specific purpose of such a meeting was to ascertain from the Negro clergy their concept of this newly realized freedom and their subsequent role in the future. Attending that meeting were several members of the clergy of Savannah. During that meeting, there were two questions raised, the answers to which are just as relevant and meaningful in 2003 as they were in 1865. The General asked the black clergy to define for him their concept of freedom and their understanding of slavery.

Their definition of freedom and understanding of slavery is of the most profound essence ever articulated by anyone for whom freedom is appreciated.

The Reverend Garrison Frazier emerged as the spokesperson for the delegation of black preachers, the following is his definition: "Slavery is receiving by irresistible power the work of another man and not by his consent. The freedom, as I understand it, is promised by the Proclamation as taking us from under the yoke of bondage, and placing us where we could reap the fruit of our own labor, take care of ourselves, and assist the government in maintaining our freedom." Given the advantage of twentieth-century education and technology, a more specific and definitive answer could not be offered or more effectively articulated than those advanced by Reverend Frazier in 1865.

The term freedom, and the pursuit of, has taken on a diversity of approaches since time immemorial. At various junctures in human history, freedom has been exploited and utilized as the freedom to destroy freedom. Therefore, the very freedom for which one has given his life has been utilized to rob another of that freedom. However, this concept of freedom is antithetical to the freedom that is inherently implied and involves social responsibility and ethical behavior. Freedom to destroy freedom is anarchy rather than social and ethical freedom. Freedom is not only a status bequeathed to humanity by divine decree; it is the ideal aspiration of those who enjoy it and to make it a reality for all people. This chapter concerns itself with the concept of freedom as it is written and espoused in the life and works of David Walker.[101]

The socio-cultural milieu that produced David Walker was such that rendered one a slave on the one hand while on the other hand another enjoyed freedom. The social imbalance and the lack of the equitable distribution of economic wealth caused David Walker's appalling disdain for the status quo in America: half free and half slave. Walker's concept of freedom emerges out of his understanding of divine justice, the Declaration of Independence, and the Constitution of the United States of America.

It is appalling and detestable that the age of progress for one color of people ushers in an age of repression, subjugation, and slavery for another color of people. The European efforts at revitalizing the economic life of Europe, coupled with a new concept of individual freedom and progress, ultimately led to the commercial revolution and exploitation of fellow human beings. Among these freedoms of movement and new opportunities for economic wealth was the birth of the American Institution of modern slavery. Walker was born during this era of slavery, in 1785.

The writing of Walker is limited to one document; The Appeal of 1829. However, there are several articles and quotes from sermons. or speeches, reprinted in Freedom's Journal. To understand and appreciate

---

[101] W, E, B. DuBois. Suppression of the African Slave Trade to the United States of America. (Cambridge: Russell & Russell. 1898), pp. 23-30.

Walker's concept of freedom, one must first explore and understand his concept of slavery and his continued disdain for the system as it lived in America. In September of 1829, there appeared the first edition of <u>Walker's Appeal</u>. The <u>Appeal</u> sets forth Walker's concept of God, his theology, his understanding of history, and his concept of justice and equality. Also, the Appeal explicitly reveals Walker's abhorrence of the inconsistency between the American slave system and democracy and Christianity.

In the early 1820's Walker moved from his native North Carolina to Boston, Massachusetts where he began to associate with learned men, and he used these associations and influences to promote the freedom of the slave. His theme was essentially the same: slavery degrades man and renders him less than a person, comparatively less than the dumb farm and domestic animals. Because of the slave master's perception of the lack of equal inherent worth and dignity of the slave, the master would never, of his own volition, set the slave free. This conviction developed out of Walker's visual inspection and experience of the existential situation of the slave. In light of the existence and reality of slavery, he vocally advocated that the slave must get his freedom by any means necessary, at whatever cost in blood, because death is better than life under such conditions.

The concert of this chapter is to arrive at what was for Walker, his concept of freedom. The initial hurdles and difficulties lie in his failure to articulate that concept in a sentence, or in precise temps. However, his Aval is saturated with language that cites historical, religions and political realities and situations that allow one to peer into his psyche and determine his motivations for freedom; freedom for Walker was just the opposite of slavery, given some deletions and additions. For Walker, slavery was morally and ethically wrong, and he resorted to the bases of the Judeo-Christian religion as an approach to demonstrating his disdain for the system. The appearance of the <u>Appeal</u> in 1829 sets in motion Walker's militant anti-slavery crusade. The theme that runs the course of Walker's writings is freedom. Slavery was a political blunder, a social injustice, and a moral dilemma for America. Thus for Walker, the slaveholders were cruel and murderous and inflicted inhumane burdens upon the slaves. In the true sense of the word, enemy, the slave master was the enemy of the slave by nature. Walker was of the conviction that "the greatest aspiration of the slave master was to keep ... us in abject ignorance and wretchedness." The "us" here implies Walker's total identification with the slave, although he was born a free man.

During the course of Walker's obscure life before the publishing and distribution of his Appeal. Walker's own testimony is that he had traveled quite extensively over the United States, thus he was aware of and had insight into the horrors of slavery as experienced by the slave. His assessment of slaves, or the opposite of freedom, was that they had no peer, either historically or contemporaneously. The existence of slavery created a further paradox for Walker in the sense that a so-called Christian nation allowed a form of subjugation of one human being to another human being predicated upon the perception of social inferiority. Therefore, America becomes a nation of hypocrites in theory and in practice who suppresses the worth and dignity of one person and elevates the inherent worth and dignity of other people. For Walker, this was an amazing paradox on the one hand, but it was a reality with which Walker was close to dealing by using every ounce of his physical strength and intellectual acumen. In the thought of Walker, there was the prevailing concept and accompanying understanding that God is just and that He is always on the side of the underdog, and that ultimately truth would win out over lies, justice over injustice, and, that the God of the oppressed people would visit on behalf of His oppressed people.

Walker's conception of freedom is expressed in the totality of his writings, speeches, and sermons, rather than in one or two specific sentences or statements. The core of Walker's rhetoric and accompanying social efforts are captured, in essence, in solve of his famous expressions: "We must and shall be free ... in spite of you." (the slave system), "and wo, wo, will be to you if we have to obtain our freedom by fighting." Therefore, one is led, inevitably, to raise that piercing question, what is freedom for Walker? Is freedom for him essentially commensurate with that freedom as expressed by the delegation of black clergy persons who met with General Sherman at Savannah, Georgia in 1865? Is freedom for Walker tantamount to the right of the oppressor to oppress the oppressed? Is freedom a quality of life or a quantity of life reserved for one race of people and denied to another race? Is freedom primarily a political and social gift bequeathed to one by the State? Or is freedom a uniquely human quality or a state of being to which one is automatically entitled, and upon whom God genetically bestows it, by virtue of human existence?[102]

Obviously, these questions were foremost in the mind and thoughts of David Walker as he wrestled with the slave tragedy of the nation. If Walker's answers to the questions raised above are a resounding no, then his concept of freedom is diametrically opposed to those concepts espoused by the slaveocracy. However, truth is truth; reality is reality, and freedom is seen through the eye of the beholder. The reality of such an understanding of life is further asserted and demonstrated through the political and social behavior of the slave master. While one segment of America was in a vigorous struggle to eternally alter its political status, another segment was also vigorously engaged in both a political and social struggle to perpetuate the slave status of blacks. The so-called dominant society was, in a sense, oblivious to the subtle and insidious developments and freedom struggle of a Walker. They were too involved in the Westward movement, manifest destiny, economic wealth, and, the development of the political institution to take serious note of the possibility that any black man was capable. intellectually or politically, of mounting a viable campaign against the "Peculiar Institution." The inherent motivation and drive of a significant segment of the white American psyche dictated that it was consistent with the divine plan that America becomes

---

[102] The Appeal. "Preamble", pp. 3-4.

the Promised Land for white people. It is out of this level of self-centeredness, and the white man's sense of superiority over blacks that catapulted David Walker into the forefront of the black liberation struggle.

His <u>Appeal</u> of 1829 shocked the consciousness of white America and caused many to take note of the uncomfortable degree with which the slave endured the "Peculiar Institution." The year 1829 was a year of colossal strides for Walker and a forward thrust for freedom. He had now moved from Wilmington, North Carolina to Boston, Massachusetts, where he did his writings and gave his speeches on liberation and freedom. The core of Walker's argument against human slavery was based on his understanding of God and servitude. In the preamble to the Appeal, Walker appeals to human reason and logic and takes the position that "God made man serve Him alone, and that man should have no other Lord or Lords but Himself ... that God Almighty is the sole proprietor or master of the whole human family ..." Walker's understanding of God was predicated upon his theology of the Christian religion; based upon his theological position, which accentuated the justice, righteousness, and goodness of God. Walker was immediately confronted with a theological and divine inconsistency. This obvious inconsistency was a problem in his perception of theodicy, on his understanding of the deity, sovereignty, and justice of God. His dilemma was to justify his perception of the goodness of God in the light of the existential reality of slavery. Slavery was running rampant in God's world without any significant effort on God's part to immediately eradicate such evil from His world. The prevailing question for Walker was: "If God is all-powerful and all-merciful, why doesn't He eliminate evil in the World?" The theological and intellectual divine-human dialogue resumes with the inherent pessimism and subsequent questions of God's ability on the one hand and God's will on the other hand.[103] If God is able to rid the world of the evil of slavery, and chooses not, then He obviously is unmerciful. If He cannot, then He is obviously limited in his power. For Walker, this was an amazing theological paradox. Walker resolved this paradoxical dilemma by asserting the goodness, power, and justice of God in the world in spite of those horrors endured in light of the slave system. By affirming these attributes of God, Walker was affirming a viable force in black liberation, God. Rather than hold God totally and absolutely responsible for the long history of slavery in America, Walker posits the significance of a divine-human enterprise, God and man working together in the business of human freedom.

Walker's refusal to indict God in the face of surmounting odds was a significant decision for Walker and for the slave community. Therefore, the foundation stone of hope, upon which black religion stood, was left intact by Walker's affirmation of the goodness, mercy, justice, and the all-powerful nature of God. In the development of arrival at that juncture in his experience, Walker understood the virtual political and economic powerlessness of the slave; and, to rob the

---

[103] The Appeal. "Preamble", pp. 3-4.

slave of his faith in God would have been tantamount to utter chaos and despair in the light of the onslaught of slavery. Walker's concept of freedom arises out of his understanding of the nature of God's goodness and fairness. His concept of freedom was congruent with God's concept of freedom, in the sense that God did not dichotomize between the spiritual and the physical. God's concept of freedom was found in His actions in history, beginning with the liberation of Israel from Egypt and His continual involvement in the liberation of persons from systematic and systematic forms of oppression.[104]

The history of God's relationship with man reflects His involvement in liberation and freedom. Walker agreed that God created man to worship Him alone and that God did not create man to form a master-slave relationship, rather, that man was created by God to be free, and that out of that creation, God and man formed a relationship of dependence and interdependence. God, however, initiates this relationship, and man uses his free will to respond to the divine initiative. Thus, the relationship is more than a slave-master relationship; it is a relationship in which the more powerful treats the less powerful as a totally free being with the freedom of choice in his destiny. This, in essence, is Walker's concept of freedom. While Walker's key components argue for freedom from the perspective of a non-human being and transfer the relationship of that perspective to the

---

[104] Louis Filler. Crusade Against Slavery, 1830-1860. (New York: Harper & Company, 1960), p. 23.

human, he does not invalidate his argument. Rather, Walker conscripts into service the laws of nature and nature's God to oppose what he understood as a grave abuse and denial of divine freedom to all of God's human creatures. This abuse of divine justice was so evident for Walker that he insists that its eradication depends on human-divine efforts. Walker's strong religious stance was a continual motivating force in his crusade for freedom. In Louis Filler's work, entitled, "<u>The Crusade Against Slavery</u>," hints that Walker responded to the issue of slavery only from the perspective of wrongness or on moral grounds. But is evident through the discourse of the <u>Appeal</u> that Walker's thoughts were deeply rooted in religion. His appreciation for Bishop Richard Allen of the African Methodists Episcopal Church and Walker's references to Allen's position on the colonizing of Africans in Liberia validates the role of religion and the influence of a religious leader in his life and thoughts.

Walker's concept of freedom was not only concerned with the freedom of the salve, but also with the ultimate freedom of America. Slavery of blacks was also slavery for the slave master. For one cannot enslave another human being without experiencing a certain degree of slavery himself. While the slavery experienced by the slave master was not physical, social, and political, he nonetheless, experienced a deeper and a more agonizing form of slavery, the slavery of mind, and consciousness. This torn of slavery was inescapable and inevitable to the practitioner as long as he was guilty of perpetrating another, human slavery. Slavery of mind and of consciousness could not be abandoned at bedtime, at parties, and during religious functions; this was a stigma attached to the perpetrator that tended to accompany him as an omnipresent reality.[105] Therefore, to further sensitive the slave master to the necessity of liberating the slave, Walker appealed to the social, moral, and religious consciousness of the slave master. The prevailing motive was to show the oppressor that his total freedom was interlocked, interconnected, intertwined, and inextricably bound to the freedom of the oppressed. Walker was of the conviction that one could not enslave another without being enslaved himself. The very rhetorical questions raised by Henry Clay of Kentucky and cited by Walker in the Appeal, further authenticated the slavery of mind and consciousness realized by the slaveholders. During a speech delivered by Henry Clay on December 21, 1816, he asked "… did I ever lose any opportunity to advance the fame, honor, and prosperity of this State and the Union?" Clay's question reflects a sense of misery and political failure, and further testifies to the slavery systems that deprived a segment of fellow human beings of freedom while using his diplomatic and political tact to ensure that very freedom to another. Walker's reply to Clay's question was a resounding no![106]

David Walker's Appeal was one of the most appealing approaches to sensitizing the black community to the true nature and root causes of the "Peculiar Institution"

---

[105] The Appeal, Article IV, pp. 56-57.
[106] Ibid., pp. 50-51.

on the one hand, and on the other hand, it prepared the blacks to seek their freedom by whatever means necessary. Any means necessary leaves to the individual a degree of discretion to develop approaches to freedom that seems advantageous to him. Walker was not given the same revolutionary approaches as Nat Turner and Marcus Garvey; however, he was nonetheless overcome by revolutionary fervor and prolifically articulated the level and degree of his commitment to freedom. Walker did not dichotomize human liberation from spiritual liberation. He was of the conviction that wan was a composite whole that was not created to experience only fragments of freedom. Freedom for Walker was not a result of the compassion, sympathy, and actions of a benevolent human slaveholder; rather it is given by God. Therefore, slaves should assert themselves and realize their freedom instead of expecting the slaveholder to emancipate them. "Should tyrants ... emancipate any of you, remember that your freedom is your natural right." Because freedom is a natural right, the slave is not to expect it from another man, neither is the man to be thanked for freedom. Rather, when freedom is realized, "Thank the Holy Ghost."

There is hardly a word spoken by Walker, a speech delivered, or a sermon given that is void of the connotations of freedom. Freedom was an ever-present obsession, a driving force, and an eternal ambition of David Walker. He utilized every forum and opportunity available to him to keep the American conscious that the nation was not actualizing the core tenets of the Christian religion as long as she allowed slavery to show its ugly head in a so-called Christian society.¹⁰⁷ While delivering a speech at a public dinner in Boston, Massachusetts in 1828, Walker castigates the idea of the attempted forced consistency between slavery and Christianity. Freedom's Journal printed excerpts of the speech given at a dinner honoring Prince Abdul Rahaman, in its October 24, 1828 issue. During the toasts, David Walker took advantage of another opportunity to keep blacks aware of the present situation and to further humiliate the slaveholder: "Our worthy guest ... who was torn from his country, religion and friends, and in the very midst of Christians, doomed to perpetual tough unlawful bondage, may God enable him to obtain so much of the reward of his labor, as may purchase the freedom of his offspring."

When one places the system of slavery in juxtaposition to the idea and reality of freedom experienced by the slav'e master, one could experience less difficulty in arriving at Walker's concept of freedom. For Walker, freedom was minus the state of the slaves in America. Based on his position in his writings, freedom was the very opposite of slavery, plus more. Walker not only talked about social, political, and economic freedom; he also talked about and strove for liberation from the socio-cultural and mental concepts held by whites as to the inherent worth and dignity of the slave.

Walker argued for a totally different perception of the black man in the minds of whites.¹⁰⁸ The underlying

---

[107] Walker's Appeal, Garnet's Address. pp. 81-82.
[108] Freedom's Journal. October 24. 1829, pp. 8-9.

motive and ultimate goal was that treatment would reflect a radical alteration if the perception of the slaves by whites were altered. Walker is quite specific in Article I of his Appeal where he cites the perceptions of other races of men as men, and therefore, they qualify for freedom. The perception of their manhood was the primary basis for freedom; therefore, if blacks are not men, they are brutes and do not qualify for freedom. Walker was aware of the necessity of an altered perception of the slave if years of subjugation were to change. Slavery and subjugation were based upon the slaveholder's inherent feelings of the slaves as being inferior to the slaveholder. These feelings were deeply ingrained into the social consciousness of those who were slaveholders; and, when men are perceived as unequal, the logical consequences are unequal relationships and treatments.

Walker's primary approach to freedom was to identify the obstacles that stood in the way and blocked the avenues of freedom. In the Appeal, Walker cites four core causes of the "wretchedness" of the slave's situation:"1. Our wretchedness in consequence of slavery (Article I); 2. Our wretchedness in consequence of ignorance (Article II); 3. Our wretchedness in consequence of the preachers of tire religion of Jesus Christ (Article III); 4. Our wretchedness is a consequence of the colonizing plan (Article IV). In these four (4) articles, Walker articulates the root causes of both the institution of slavery, its lifeblood, and the rationale was not created within a vacuum and, therefore, its longevity was void of a vacuum. There were social, economic, religious, political, and immoral foundations upon which slavery stood and, to rid the nation of the horrors of slavery, there was the necessity to attack the system at its roots. The Appeal does attack the system of slavery in both a patriotic and ethical sense. Walker does not seek to emancipate the slave; he seeks to emancipate America. Based upon Walker's sense of patriotism and love for America, he saw not only the slave as being bound and robbed of his self-worth, but America was also bound by a sense of guilt and immorality. Had it been economically feasible for America to realize her economic and social goals without slavery, she would have done so, but because of the opportunity to get a cheap labor supply, the slave was exploited in spite of the clear inconsistency between slavery and Christianity. Thus, in the efforts to justify the slave system, the slave was looked upon and treated as unequal. It was, therefore, justifiable to hold in chattel slavery unequal.

The freedom theme permeates the writings of David Walker. In his <u>Appeal</u>, he sets out to identify the root causes for the denial of freedom to the slave. He does this by specifically naming the origin, practice, and perpetuation of slavery in the American Colonies. Slavery is the monster and the promoters and feeders of the monster are those who reap unjust monetary benefits from slave labor. Walker saw slavery as a brutal system and the slave as the most dehumanized person in the world. "But, we (colored people) and our children are brutes!! And of course, are, and out to be slaves to the American people and their children forever!! To dig their mines and work their farms; and thus, go on enriching them, from one generation to another with our blood and our tears!!!!" The above-cited quote is Walker's sarcasm reflected at the highest level of criticism. Freedom, for Walker, was the equal treatment of blacks, as was true in the case of whites. When Walker reflected upon his travels over the United States, and his extensive readings of the histories of Greece, Rome, Great Britain, and the Jews and of other peoples of the earth, all were seen as men, though they were slaves. But what came across to Walker as being unique was the failure of the American slave society to recognize the American slave as a genuine, authentic person. Herein lays the most blatant denial of freedom. In Article I of the Appeal, Walker attacks the slave mentality of the American people (the slave masters and supporters of the slave system) for their perception of the slave, and the assumption that the slave was satisfied to exist under the dehumanized working and living conditions of "wretchedness and misery." Freedom in the thought of David Walker was the recognition by others that blacks were human beings, equal in inherent worth and dignity to all other human beings, and accorded equal respect and appreciation as all other humans. The great task of Walker was not only to win the freedom of speech, freedom of travel, freedom to work, and receive just compensation for their work, but to force the American society to confess to the human equality of blacks.[109] The denial of freedom to the slave was based primarily upon the fallacious and artificial social and biological

---

[109] The Appeal. P. 7.

assumptions of the Negroes inherent inferiority. Freedom for Walker is the opportunity of the slaves to develop to their maximum potential the God-given talents of each individual.

Martin Luther's "Open Letter to the Christian Nobility of the German Nation," is reechoed in <u>Walker's Appeal</u>. As Luther launches righteous indignation and a Christian radicalism against the oppressors of his people, Walker also resorts to a radical approach to address the beleaguered slaves of America in a last-ditch effort to redeem the slaves in America and, ultimately, to save America. To save America, Walker deemed it necessary and appropriate to alter the religious, social, and civil orders of American society. Walker did not envision the salvation of America without redeeming the slaves. For Walker, there was an interconnectedness between slavery and America so that one could not realize its potential without the other. With this deep sense of mission, Walker understood himself as being in a direct league with God to rid the nation of its greatest and most debilitating social ill. For Walker to become vocally and literally immersed in the political battles of his day places him on the level with Luther and other revolutionary agitators and reformers of history. In the messianic role, he subjected himself to the full punishment of the laws of the Land. This is essentially the lot of Walker, who, while his contributions to black freedom are equally significant to blacks as Luther's contributions to Protestant Christianity, Luther is hailed as a hero, while Walker has been shamefully neglected by church historians. Yet, his political genius and social involvement, coupled with his zeal for freedom, catapults him into the limelight of the freedom struggle in America.

The genius of Walker is further appreciated in the first article of the <u>Appeal</u>, entitled, "Our Wretchedness in Consequence of Slavery," in which he does a comparison to slavery as documented in history. When he compared American Slavery to slavery in history, he concluded that America was guilty of the cruelest, most degrading, and dehumanizing form of slavery the world over. Walker does not glorify slavery in any form, regardless of the perpetrator's frequent ulterior motives and overt displays of humanitarian gestures as an effort to suggest that slavery was an institution to be desired or promoted among civilized men. The aspect of American slavery that appalled Walker was that it denied the Negroes' inherent self-worth and questioned his humanity. Walker easily understood but did not agree with the insidious and underlying rationale of the slave master for denying the slave's humanity. To invalidate the Negro's humanity, it was necessary to establish valid grounds for denying the Negro his freedom.

Walker argued for the inherent worth and dignity of the Negro based upon the common origin of all people, whose origin is in God. Therefore, freedom is not a state, nor a status bequeathed by the State. Rather, God bequeaths freedom by virtue of one's biological birth. This approach to dealing with the issue by Walker gets at the core of freedom and challenges one human being's right to hold another as a slave.

Freedom is the full pursuit of one's goals, aspirations, movements, expressions, involvements, beliefs, and, the opportunity to work and realize due and just compensation for labor, to own property, and to receive equal treatment of taxation and representation before the Congress and the courts of law. Slavery was the exact opposite of those stipulations of freedom, which translated into an advantage for the slave owner and a disadvantage for the slave. Movement without obstruction, thinking and acting out behavior based upon one's thinking, responding to one's own personal social needs and aspirations, and contributing to the general welfare and progress of the nation is the sum total of freedom as was understood by Walker. Obviously, in the mind of the slaveholder, this level of creative thinking was too far advanced thinking for both free blacks and blacks who were yet experiencing the bitter pains of slavery. In a sense, David Walker's blatant challenge to the status quo of slavery was a more direct and devastating attack on slavery than was Robert Alexander Young's <u>Ethiopian Manifesto</u>, also published in 1829.

Young's <u>Manifesto</u> had as its core concern the freedom of the slave, as did Walker's <u>Appeal</u>, both of which defended the black man's rights based upon universal freedom. However, Young's literary approach to the resolution of the dilemma of black slavery differed that Walker in that he saw the black man's freedom becoming a reality only through the efforts of blacks. More specifically, Young placed the responsibility of winning freedom squarely on the shoulders of black people. David Walker, on the other hand, strongly places God and man in a divine-human enterprise fighting for the freedom of the slave.

Young's position was totally a human venture and minus the divine elements, while Walker's deep religious orientation places him in a totally opposite position and approach to the freedom struggle. The crucial ingredient to social progress and individual freedom was free access to equal education. For Walker education was the opposite of ignorance, the difference between fortune and misfortune, and the dividing line between slavery and freedom. The educational achievements that translated into the erection of the pyramids of Egypt, "sons of Africa, or of Ham" directly contributed to the turning of the channel of the Nile River, and the ultimate glory and grandeur of Greece and Rome.

Unfortunately, this wisdom that originated among the "sons of Africa, or of Ham" had not been allowed to flow continually to the "sons of Africa, or of Ham" whose misfortune was indefinite slavery in America. In Article II of Walker's Appeal, there is a direct correlation between the slave's wretchedness in America and the slave master's concerted efforts to withhold from the slave the insights that come with education.

The slaves' state of educational ignorance is the total responsibility of the slave master who did not use the God-given opportunity to educate the slave in religion and in the sciences of Africa and Europe. For Walker, this was an abdication of responsibility and dereliction of divine duty. Therefore, the Negroes now plunged into ignorance ten thousand times more intolerable than they were in their native Africa. Thus, the rationale that slavery was a great school on the slave's road to civilization had a specific day-to-day curriculum without a specific graduation day. At this juncture, Walker refuses to place the total responsibility for the slave's ignorance on the shoulders of the slave. The consequences of the slave's ignorance deprived him of the ability to think of social systems and political strategy, as his oppressors were able to think and strategize. This does not suggest that Walker perceived the slave as being inherently and biologically inferior to the oppressors; rather it suggests that the lack of exposure to education itself was the chief debilitating factor.

The removal of the veil of ignorance and equal exposure to the advantages of education are critical milestones on the slave's road to freedom. While the ignorance among the slaves was widespread across the United States of America, it was in the southern and western states of the nation that ignorance was the most obvious and profoundly pronounced. For Walker, the opposite of ignorance is freedom. The wretchedness into which the slave had fallen is due to ignorance, not on the part of the slave, but by a clever design of the oppressor. The veil of ignorance not only robs man of the knowledge of what freedom really is, but it also stands as a roadblock to facilitating his efforts to achieve that freedom. Walker was keenly aware that the oppressor realized the debilitating effect of ignorance, and he was also aware of the oppressor's commitment to perpetuating the status of ignorance among the oppressed. By perpetuating the status of ignorance among the slaves, the oppressor found a degree of legitimacy for the unequal treatment of the slave.

Walker, however, extends his perception of the effects of ignorance in his assertion that "... ignorance is the mother of treachery and deceit" that tends to gnaw at the "very vitals" of a person. He asserts that while the oppressor's commitment is that of utilizing ignorance as a tool for perpetuating slavery, the oppressor is also a victim of his own device. Walker appeals to the human consciousness of the oppressor in suggesting that ignorance's ugly face is seen by those who are human beings and not by tyrants, who can feel for a fellow creature. He specifically posits that tyrants are less than human beings, or, at least, incapable of feeling like a human being. Walker is not degrading the worth and dignity of the slave master, rather he places himself in the arena of ignorance alongside the ignorant slave. This brings out of Walker his conviction that to diminish a person is to diminish one's self, for he felt that one cannot enslave another without enslaving oneself. The slave conditions in the Southern and Western United States, from which Walker had fled in 1826, did not alter their social and political goals of Walker after he relocated to Boston, Massachusetts. He became involved in a black Methodist church, and an influential supporter of Freedom's Journal, and made himself available for speeches and forums designed to advance the causes of freedom of the slave. In the early 1800s the slave issue was the subject of the church to the social halls of freemasonry, and in those societies considered clandestine by the white power structure of that era.

Nevertheless, the commitment and zeal with which the opponents of slavery advanced their cause persisted in some of the most provocative languages and is reflected in prolific literature. David Walker was one of the vocal supporters of the cause of black freedom and whose appeal encouraged continual resistance among the slaves. Walker's position on the issue of slavery had an impact on the social conditions in the North as it did on the conditions of the South. Vincent Harding identifies the resulting effects of the joining of the forces of those in the North who protested against Northern racism and Southern discrimination against the slave. He sees the joining of the Northern and Southern forces to combat the common enemy to freedom as an effort to ensure the continued protection of those fugitive slaves from the South. These efforts of the Northern and Southern liberation movements were of an interdependent nature in the sense that the Northern groups became active in protecting the haven in the North.

David Walker represents one of the early voices of protest against slavery in the United States. Therefore, he fits quite well into what Harding calls "The Great Traditions of Black Protest." For Walker, the tradition was not simply the passing on from one generation to the other the useless and worthless ideas and ideologies of the past, rather it is the ability to, and the capacity for translating history's failures and triumphs into positive approaches to enhancing the quality of life for the slave. The black religious tradition has been called and treated as a religion of protest. While black religion is reflected throughout history as being actively involved in the social and political protests against slavery, black religion is not single-focused historically. Rather, black religion has been multifaceted, which has given it the flexibility to include a protest against every form of indignity perpetrated upon human beings that held the possibility of degrading them spiritually and socially. Walker refused, through his behavior and writings, to dichotomize man, rather he viewed humankind holistically.

By the year 1828, Walker had reached a level of notoriety that he was now being invited to use the General Colored Association of Massachusetts as a forum to articulate his anti-slavery strategy. Walker saw tremendous possibilities inherent within the black community and utilized his writing and vocal skills to further sensitize black people to their inevitable role and to the invaluable contribution they were to make in alleviating the conditions of slavery in the United States. The insights of David Walker into the core problems of the black struggle for freedom provided him with a level of social, political, and economic perceptivity that uniquely prepared him as a mobilizing force against slavery. Walker's initial effort was to mobilize the black community by speaking to the need for political and social organizations within the black community. Approaching the formation of organizational structures was an invaluable strategy to foster the mind of cohesiveness needed within the black community and was a prerequisite to winning the political and social battles that led to black freedom in America.

Freedom to think and act rationally; freedom to identify with the real and advantageous goals and aspirations of the slave, and the perpetual sense of interdependence are what Walker saw as real freedom. By design, the slave had not been oriented to perceive reality in that sense. Rather, the slave was a victim of white perpetuated ignorance that he would turn on his own people to defend the slave master, as was seen in the Kentucky incident where a female slave assisted a wounded slave trader who had been attacked by a freedom-loving slave. Walker saw the attacking of the slave trader as another opportunity to win his freedom, had an ignorant slave woman fully understood the plight of the slave.

David Walker was able to perceive a deeper significance in the Kentucky incident than was seen by the politicians and slave traders. His level of perception was raised to the level of divinity where he saw this as a divinely-orchestrated, existential moment, taking advantage of such a moment would advance the cause of black freedom. However, because of the level of ignorance experienced by the slave, he was not able to take proper advantage of a divine situation. Walker was so engrossed in the freedom struggle that he ventured to compare the slave and the slave master to God and mammon. Obviously, the opposite of God is mammon, sin, evil, inhumanity, and slavery.

The specific admonition of Walker is that each slave should have joined in league with God to fight against the forces of evil. Article II, of the <u>Appeal,</u> is Walker's obvious effort to sensitize the slave, who has fallen under the wretchedness of the wrath of ignorance, to recognize the appearances of the divine opportunities to win their freedom.

The essential argument of Walker was the reality of slavery in America, half slave and half free. He also acted out of the reality that the slave would never become free if he waits on the goodness and benevolence of the slave master. For as freedom was an eternal longing and aspiration of the slave perpetual slavery was the eternal longing and aspiration of the slave master. In all actuality, slavery and freedom are of equal existence. for as long as there has been a slave; there have been overt and covert efforts to be free. Rebellion is uniquely a part of the human species! While cows, birds, and other creatures have expressed a desire to be free of cages, traps, and other places of confinement, never has there been a creature of history that has resorted to an equivalent behavior as has mankind to win his own freedom. The history of the human family is specifically and impressively punctuated by its revelations and rebellions to attain freedom. Walker existed in an environment heavily saturated with cruelty, atrocities, and the denial of freedom to the slave. Hypothetically, suppose the profit margin of slavery was non-existent; suppose that slaves were not held to gratify the sexual pleasure of their owners; suppose there had been available another means of entertainment would there not have been an era of human slavery in America?

The answers advanced to these hypothetical questions will depend largely upon those from whom we solicit those answers. However, given the nature and obvious maltreatment of blacks throughout American History, I am left to conjecture that the dominant society would have found other approaches to elevate its level of importance and stature. Walker felt so strongly about the evil and benefit motives for chattel slavery, that he was convinced that human slavery was an inevitable consequence of ignorance. Walker conjectured further that because of the mental, economic and political composition of" white America, the slave master would not stop short of dethroning the system of justice and equality to promote his individual cause if it were possible. Walker raises the theological question as to the nature of the slave master: "Are they as good by nature as we are or not?" While he does not pursue the theological question to a biblical conclusion, he asserts that the actions testify to the contrary. Walker's deep commitment to liberty, justice, and the total freedom of the slave, found for him a basis in God as a liberator. Therefore, if God is always involved in the business of human liberation, for a human being to think and behave contrary to God's behavior places man in a position opposed to God. Walker's stunning charges of man's actions as being inconsistent with God were directed toward the white Christian community of America. Walker does not limit his criticisms to the white community: he also launches a severe charge against the black community, whom he saw as portraying a level of ignorance and practicing a degree of treachery against fellow slaves that benefited the slave master over the slave. It is in that sense that Walker appeals to the black community to become involved in educating themselves as a positive approach to their own freedom. The theme that runs throughout the course of Article II is that the opposite of freedom is ignorance. He felt very strongly that one cannot be educated and a chattel slave in America synonymously.

Was the sum total of Walker's argument for freedom based primarily on the realities of slavery and educational ignorance, or did he perceive other significant factors that contributed equally to the dilemma of slavery in the United States? To the latter question, the answer is a resounding yes! For Walker perceived there to be an even deeper reality that stood in the way of Freedom's progress. Walker perceived a degree of apathy among the slaves on the one hand, and on the other hand apathy from the slave master. While there were isolated reports of benevolent whites that introduced their slaves to education, it was not a common practice nor an aspiration of the majority of whites to develop an educated slave. Walker's commitment to freedom as expressed in the Appeal tends to sensitize the slave to the African traditional zeal for freedom. The apathy reflected in the slave's daily lives in America was not typical of his cultured experience in his native land. John Barfat, a slave ship captain, penned in his journal in 1701 the slave's struggle for freedom when he recorded, "We stood in arms, firing on the revolted slaves, of whom we killed some and wounded many ... and many of the most mutinous leapt overboard, and drowned themselves in the ocean with many resolutions."

Rebellion, revolution, and abolition of slavery, not apathy, ignorance, and passivity, have been the rallying cries of the slaves since the first capture in Africa of a person destined for a slave plantation in the "New World." For Walker, the socio-cultural settings, the political and economic realities of slavery, coupled with the dehumanizing process and strategy of the slave master robbed the slave of much of his will to live in America. With the obvious impossibility of freedom, many slaves succumbed to the apathy and lethargy to which the slave master had led them. Walker's <u>Appeal</u>, as he stated near the beginning of his work, "was to awaken in the breasts of my afflicted, degraded and slumbering brethren, a spirit of inquiry and investigation respecting our miseries and wretchedness in this Republican Land of Liberty."

While Walker's concept of freedom involves the freedom of thought that translates into the positive growth and development of the slave's inherent potential, he saw these possibilities being actualized through a complete reorientation of the American psyche. Walker addresses himself to the process through which the American system of slavery and the slave master must journey if true freedom of the slave is to become a reality. He sets forth his position in ten steps or ten considerations: (1) Degradation of blacks by white racists must end; (2) Divine judgment on whites unless they repent; (3) Blacks must end their complicity through open resistance; (4) Black solidarity: (5) Blacks must resist the efforts of colonization; (6) Blacks must gain education as a weapon in the struggle for freedom; (7) The possibility of a new society of peace and justice could emerge if whites abandon racism and avarice; (8) The need for a Protestant Christian religion to undergird the black struggle for freedom; (9) The possibility of his death through assassination; (10) and a repeated sense of solidarity among the brothers and sisters of slavery.

The ten themes that run through Walker's <u>Appeal</u> get at the core of what defines the prerequisites to freedoms. The topics articulated in the ten themes of the <u>Appeal</u> specifically define his approaches to freedom and suggest that freedom's reality is not experienced without human-divine help, or human-divine participation.[110] This brings out of Walker his deep theological orientation of a divine-human enterprise in the liberation of the slave. The social and religious nomenclature of the ten themes is reflective of a champion of freedom who faces the reality of eventual futility if the appropriate forces, God or man, abandon the plight of the slave. Walker's solicitation of and resorting to the aid of the transcendent in the fight for freedom is not a denial of the slave's role in winning freedom, rather it is a reflection of his theological position of God's imminence in the earth and His transcendence above His creation. Of the ten themes that permeate Walker's <u>Appeal</u>, four of them are the responsibilities of whites, five are the responsibilities

---

[110] Vincent Harding. <u>There Is A River</u>. (New York: Harcourt Brace and Jovanovich, 1981), pp. 3-5.

of blacks, and one is the responsibility of God. Why are five of them the responsibility of blacks, four the responsibility of whites, and only one the responsibility of God? For Walker, this was not inconsistent with freedom's struggle or the behavior of God. He reserves the meeting out of justice for God, which will come, and can only be prevented if both blacks and whites adhere to God's demand for justice. The black community has a responsibility of solidifying themselves, and the white community has the responsibility of abandoning racism. Divine justice would come only if whites refused to participate in the mission of liberation. He was not denying the reality of the slave master's commitment to slavery; rather he endeavored to appeal to the possible moral and ethical consciousness of an evil tyrant.

As David Walker delved more deeply into religion, he saw freedom as a fight in which God himself was involved. In that sense, and imbued with that theological conviction, Walker's struggle takes on an added significance that places him alongside Nat Turner, which adds to it a messianic fervor. Whatever there was about the social, political, and religious behavior of David Walker, it has its origins in his sensitivity and deep commitment to the human predicament of slavery. Walker saw slavery as a human predicament that was based upon the social norms of nineteenth-century America. Society was so engrossed in the social system that permitted slavery to survive, that by the time of David Walker, slavery had become an acceptable way of life for those who realized economic wealth and for those whose social status was enhanced through the humiliation and degradation of the slave.

The role of religion in the life and behavior of Walker is significant in the sense of his frequent references to God and His role in the human struggle for freedom. Religion was a logical system of support, given its nature and role in the history of many peoples of the World. The point of departure for the black liberation struggle was the Exodus experience in the life of ancient Israel. The Exodus event was also a factor in the thoughts and actions of those who formed the Republic known as the United States of America.[111] In the thoughts of most abolitionists, slavery presented a severe obstacle to the ideas of democracy, freedom, and justice. Inherent within the Exodus theme were liberation and freedom. The discovery of America and the eventual conquest of the territory suggested to the Founding Fathers a sense of divine intervention and support on behalf of Europe. It became rather ironic quite early during the expansion westward into Missouri Territory that the "... white interpreted Promised Land" was being enlarged to include new areas where slavery's power was to be expanded. Therefore, for the slaveholder, the expansion westward beyond the Appalachians and the Mississippi River was a destiny supported by God and the white man's understanding of the Christian religion. This movement, annexation, conquest, and possession were all done in the name of religion and political greed without any serious consideration of

---

[111] Ibid., p. 89.

the non-white chattel, whose labor would enlarge the economic coffers of the slave masters. During the 1820s and 1830s, the nation had formerly committed itself to the system of Chattel slavery and was opposed to any viable efforts or persons who dared to offer a challenge. It must not be overlooked, however, that a significant number of white men were also involved in anti-slavery activities. To categorically stereotype all Pre-Civil War whites as racists and pro-slavery is to ignore a reality of abolitionist history. While slavery was conceived, promoted, and perpetuated upon blacks by whites, there were those whites at various levels of society who bitterly opposed the slave system.[112]

There were personal convictions and open opposition to slavery that emanated from both the political and religious communities. It is quite interesting that as early as 1792, the Reverend David Rice, the father of Presbyterianism in the State of Kentucky, bitterly opposed slavery, describing the system as "a perpetual war, with an avowed purpose of never making peace." He saw slavery as a system that would eventually and ultimately benefit the enemy and weaken the home front. The enemy of slavery was the freedom lover, and the home front was America. The list of anti-slavery white support includes Theodore Wright of Connecticut whose immortal words get at the core of the danger of slavery:

"And when hostilities are commenced, where will they (the slaveholders) look for auxiliaries, in such an

---

[112] Ibid., p. 76.

iniquitous warfare? Surely, no friend to freedom and justice will dare to lend his aid ...Who then can charge the Negroes with injustice, or cruelty, when they rise in all vigor of insulted nature, and avenge their wrongs. What American will not admire their exertions to accomplish their own deliverance?"

Judge Jabez Brown of Georgia was exiled to Rhode Island for his criticism of slavery and for stating that open rebellion by the slave was justifiable. Humphrey Smith of Howard County, Missouri, in 1819, was indicted by a country grand jury for making what they determined as remarks that "incited slave rebellion." In 1822, four white men were arrested and convicted for their role in the Vesey plot in South Carolina. The list of white support against slavery is inexhaustible and, therefore, it should be remembered that the total white community was not in support of slavery. This is further evidenced by the involvement of the abolitionist groups, extending from the Quakers to Garrison, Tappan, Benjamin Franklin, Benjamin Rush, John Jay, and Thomas Paine. Many years ago, Charles S. Braden suggested, "... that religion was the chief differentiating characteristic of man." He further posited that no nation of human beings or people has been found to be void of religion. Religion has played a significant role in the life of people since the advent of humankind on planet earth. To the sound of religious drums, nations have emerged, thrived and fallen. To the sound of religious drums, armies have marched, fought, and won victories. To cadences of biblical music, kings, queens, potentates, and presidents have been enthroned, coronated, and inaugurated. To the beat of religious drums, people have been treated unjustly, killed, and enslaved. In light of the voluminous feats of malevolence and benevolence done in the name of religion, what does it mean to say that religion is the chief differentiating characteristic of man? How has religion contributed to the uniqueness of man? Uniqueness refers to a single aspect of a person or a thing that makes it different from anything else in this world.[113] With that description as a working definition of uniqueness, the question is inescapable: how is man different because of his religion? Man is better and worse because of his religion, and not just religion itself. Man's religion is a subjective approach to finding meaning in his life. No religion is minus the subjective aspects and approaches to individual meaning and self-aggrandizement. Therefore, religion reflects cultural norms and standards. Religion might even border on the reflection of one's understanding of his god based upon his understanding of the culture in which he lives. Paul Tillich alludes that theology is "culturology". Thus, one's religion takes into account one's cultural experiences and practices, and those experiences and practices tend to shape and form one's external behavior and relationships with others who are a part of that culture and society. Therefore, religion determines largely the folkways and mores of the society, and, by the same token, society determines the folkways and

---

[113] Herbert Aptheker. <u>One Continual Cry: David Walker's Appeal to the Colored Citizens of the World</u>. (New York: Humanities Press, 1965), pp. 3-5.

mores of religion. Ultimately, religion and culture are interdependent and interconnected.

Hardly any living person of David Walker's era was more sensitive to and aware of this interdependence and interconnectedness between religion and society than Walker. For Walker, religion was not some aspect of humanity that could be easily detached from man and rendered unimportant in his total behavior.

Therefore, religion was not a come-and-go affair: if one is religious, it permeates the whole of his existence. The history of the black man's religion testifies, not only to its indispensable nature and role in one's life, but it also points out the obvious inconsistency between the black man's religion and white Christianity in America. Gayraud S. Wilmore is quite perceptive and relevant when lie discusses the hypocritical posture and blatant misuse of the Christian religion by the organized churches of the slave era. He suggests what he calls "the disestablishment of white Christianity soon after independence which removed the church front the center of public life." Wilmore has in mind the lessened degree of influence exerted upon society by organized white Christianity. He suggests that while white Christianity continued to "exercise a certain authority in manners and morals well into the twentieth century," its power and influence were being weakened by the gradual rise of the black church from its former clandestine existence to that of an organized religious body.

For Walker, religion as was preached by the white preachers had lost its original purpose and meaning for the slave. Article III, of his Appeal, launches a direct attack on the slave master's brand of Christianity as a cause of the wretchedness of the slave. For Walker, religion as was defined by white Christians, was one of the blatant and critical obstacles standing in the way of freedom of the slave. It is a strange irony that the very means of equal justice and fairness among religious America would be conceived and responded to as a deterrent and as a roadblock to freedom.[114] Obviously, based upon Walker's deep religious conviction, he is not necessarily denying the validity of religion, nor the positive role religion plays in life and in the history of humankind. Rather, Walker is addressing the negative direction religion has taken with the misuse by the slave master's preachers. Obviously, Walker perceived authentic Christianity as that preached by Jesus Christ and his apostles.[115]

---

[114] Gayraud S. Wilmore. Black religion and Black Radicalism. (New York: Doubleday, 19720, PP. 2-5.
[115] The Appeal., p. 35.

CHAPTER VII

AN ANALYSIS OF DAVID WALKER'S APPEAL

David Walker was born in Wilmington, North Carolina in 1785. His mother was a free black woman, but his father was a slave. Walker took on the status of his mother and based on the laws of the State of North Carolina, Walker was a free man. Walker moved from the South in the early 1800s and relocated to Boston, Massachusetts where he entered the used clothing business during the 1800s. In Boston, Walker learned to read and write, which later proved helpful to him in his clothing business. From Boston, Gayraud Wilmore posits that Walker made several trips to the South where he observed the cruelties of slavery firsthand and from those experiences, Walker developed a disdain for the slave system. In later years Walker would express his disdain in words that sounded revolutionary in nature and in tone. Wilmore further asserts that the <u>Appeal</u> was "... the most powerful piece of anti-slavery propaganda to be written by a black man."

The Appeal attracted the attention of people from a wide area of concern, both from friends and from persons such as William Lloyd Garrison and Fleury Highland Garnet. Garrison thought the Appeal to be too radical while Garnet saw it as welcome revolutionary material that led to Henry Highland Garnet's famous "Let your Motto be resistance." Garnet became a student of Walker in a theological and abolitionist sense, and would later pick up the struggle and espouse through his own anti-slavery efforts, the tenor of David Walker.[116]

Further insights will be later presented as to the efforts of Garnet's anti-slavery activities and his identification with the struggle in which Walker was involved, and additional attention will be placed on what Garnet did with what he gained from Walker.[117]

Walker's travels throughout the South provided him with a feel for the whole atrocities experienced by the slaves and first-hand knowledge of the slaves' conditions as they actually existed, and as those conditions attested to the cruelties in the lives of the slaves. Walker's observations led him to evaluate and compare slavery as was practiced in the United States with slavery as it was practiced in other civilizations, which convinced him that the form of slavery practiced in the United States was the most degrading form of slavery ever known to civilized man. It is in the Appeal that Walker

---

[116] Gayraud S. Wilmore. Black Religion and Black Radicalism. (New York: Doubleday and Company, 1972), pp. 2-5.
[117] Henry Highland Garnet. "Let Your Motto Be Resistance", in Sterling Stuckey's The Ideological Origins of Black Nationalism. (Boston: Beacon Press, 1972), pp. 18-22.

describes the slave as experiencing the most degrading set of conditions since the world began. He describes the plight of the slave as wretched, dehumanizing, abject, and wicked. While Walker does not define slavery by utilizing those specific words or tends, he leaves very little doubt in the reader's minds that freedom is the exact opposite of the lifestyle forced upon the slave by the slave system. Thus, freedom and liberation become the opposites of wretchedness, dehumanization, and the suffering of wickedness at the hands of those who subordinated another person to slave status in order to advance their own economic self-interests. Vincent Harding has posited that through Walker's efforts in the cause of freedom "the word black radicalism has become fresh." Harding further asserts that it was the relentless pursuing power of God that led both Walker and Nat Turner to the "river of struggle." Harding sees a close similarity in the points of departure between David Walker and Nat Turner in their pursuit of the liberation of the slaves. He points out that from the streets of Boston, streets built by the slave traders, to the remote countryside of Virginia, became the launch pads for liberation in the lives of Walker and Turner. Walker saw within slavery the inherent evils that allowed the slave to become a simple chattel. Therefore, if persons can become chattel as cows and hogs are, it becomes less difficult to treat them as such; and therefore, without incurring the wrath of "their God," and the wrath of society.

 Walker attacked slavery and the slave-owners from the perspective of the Christian Religion. His argument centered around the given that America declared itself to be a Christian nation which, as Walker understood Christianity, was inherently a religion whose basic tenets promoted the equality of all peoples of the earth. For Walker, slavery was wrong because it robbed the individual of certain inalienable rights, as seen in the Declaration of Independence, "... life, liberty and the pursuit of happiness."[118] Walker launched an attack, not on Christianity itself; rather his attack was focused on that brand of Christianity that allowed the slave owners and the slaves to be Christians simultaneously.

It is significant to note that David Walker was a devout Christian who understood himself as seeing the hand of God operating in the lives of peoples and nations. Walker practiced the Christian Religion and "... was a faithful member of the Methodist Church at Boston."[119] Walker was committed to God so strongly that he understood the dual role of God and man in the slave's liberation. Walker states that man ought to work with God for liberation, or he should remain a slave forever. For Walker, this was the formation of a divine-human enterprise for the good of the nation and for the slave. Walker saw an interconnection between the image of the nation and that of slavery; the image being that while the slave endured an inferior status in America, the nation, through its slave system, was having cast

---

[118] Vincent Harding. There Is A River: The Struggle for Black Freedom in America. (New York: Harcourt Brace Jovanovich, 1981), pp. 3-5.

[119] Leon F. Litwack. North of Slavery. (Chicago: The University of Chicago Press, 1961), p. 191.

upon her a negative image in the world community, which cast a dark shadow on the religion that was so central to the goals and political doctrines of America. Walker viewed slavery and Christianity as inconsistent and incompatible, and as destructive to the nation. There were, and are, those who would categorize Walker as an atheist because of his attack on Christianity. But based on his statements, which saturate the <u>Appeal</u>, there was a strong belief in God, in His justice, and in the faith that He would vindicate the slave. It was out of those experiences that Walker was moved to write, what is now known as, <u>David Walker's Appeal to the Colored Citizens of the World</u>, with special emphasis on the conditions, attitudes, and perspectives of the blacks in the United States of America.

David Walker's Appeal was both unanticipated and unwanted by the Southern aristocracy who profited from the commercial enterprise of dealing in "man-stealing" and "man-selling" and, human exploitation. The <u>Appeal's</u> initial impact on the slaveholder was that of disbelief. In his work, A Species of Property, Leon F. Litwack dealt with this degree of disbelief in the North and in the South. In addition to the consternation produced in the North by the publication and distribution of <u>Walker's Appeal</u>, C Cement Eaton points out that the South was alarmed.[120] He suggests that the alarm stemmed from an already-developed fear of slave uprisings in the South.

---

[120] Clement Eaton, "A Dangerous Pamphlet in the Old South", Journal of Southern History, 1936, p. 90.

This fear was heightened with the sudden appearance of copies of Walker's Appeal in areas across the South. Litwack also points out the potentially volatile and explosive nature of the Appeal and the South's immediate response to it. The mayor of Savannah, Georgia requested the mayor of Boston. Massachusetts, that Walker is arrested and punished, while the mayor of Richmond, Virginia reported that several copies of the Appeal had been found among and in the possession of local free slaves. The governors of Georgia and North Carolina presented copies of the Appeal to their respective legislatures for appropriate actions to be taken, while Mississippi and Louisiana enacted special legislation to deal with those in whose possession the Appeal was found. The appalling attitudes and disbelief expressed by white slave owners came in the sense that the idea had been promoted that a black person was not intellectually astute enough to produce a pamphlet in which there was articulated the plight of an oppressed people. A resultant reaction was that of anger; anger in the sense that the white system of suppression and deprivation of Negro education had been a failure as to a David Walker who proved that a black person is fully capable of being educated. The malady of Walker's articulation of the Negroes' plight and the white man's nightmare suggested to white America that the Negro does have the capacity to think and act for himself, profess data, and express himself in accurate and threatening language. The language of the Appeal was revolutionarily threatening to the point that he calls into question 'Thomas Jefferson, who drafted the Declaration of Independence. Walker's response to Jefferson's "Notes on Virginia," he wrote: "suffering will come to an end, in spite of all the Americans this side of eternity. Then we will want all the learning and talents among ourselves, and perhaps more, to govern ourselves."

In addition to the disbelief and anger aroused by the Appeal, which had been secretly smuggled into the South and was being read to illiterate slaves, there was posed the threat of self-earning which was sure death to the slave system. Herbert Aptheker in his treatment of the famous line in Walker's Appeal. "One Continual" in which Walker states "if the abomination were rightly understood, one continual cry would be raised in all parts of the confederacy and would cease only with the complete overthrow of the system of slavery in every part of the country."[121] Walker suggests that the marrows of slavery were not fully known nor understood by the majority of Americans; if so, it would not be tolerated. The Appeal was Walker's approach to informing the nation of the realities of slavery and of the adverse impact it was having on the Nation.

Vincent Harding is quite perceptive as to that aspect of Walker's message that registers a warning to the Nation of that inescapable reality that ties the Nation's future to that of the slaves' future. "I tell you Americans! That unless you speedily alter your course, you and your country are gone!" This was a gut-level the feeling of Walker and of a number of those involved in

---

[121] Herbert Aptheker. To Be Free: Studies in American Negro History. (New York: International Publishers, 1969), pp. 8-10.

abolitionist activities during this time of Walker. Herein lays the interconnectedness of the nation's destiny with that of the slaves' destiny. Hence, Walker stands within the tradition of the Biblical Prophets in which he offers America a choice between "chaos or community," for the two destinies were intertwined. While Walker offers an opportunity for repentance, he expresses a degree of pessimism that white America will pass up the opportunity for repentance and, as a result, the Nation will fall under the wrath of God. Walker's love and hope for America are further evident when he said "I hope that Americans will hear … but I am afraid that they have done us so much … so their destruction may be sure."[122]

The <u>Appeal</u> was both evolutionary and revolutionary! it was revolutionary in the sense that it reflects a long and slow developmental process; it recounts the history of black people the world over and points to their treatment from Egypt to the shores of the United States of America. It is revolutionary in the sense that it demands immediate and drastic alterations in the relationship between whites and blacks in America. The <u>Appeal</u> offered slaveholders an opportunity to respond positively to the issue of liberating the slave, which could be realized without actual bloodshed. However, if the path to liberation necessitated bloodshed, then Walker advocated winning liberation by whatever means necessary, even bloodshed. Of course, "there was

---

[122] Vincent Harding. <u>There Is A River: The Black Struggle for Freedom in America</u>. (New York: Harcourt Brace Jovanovich, 1981), pp. 3-5.

no interest," as Harding points out, "on the part of the slave owners to repent, rather they only see themselves being forced into an open rebellion and frantically prepared themselves to respond to the eventuality."[123] They did this by enacting laws, codes, and regulations to further control the slaves. To ensure that the message of enlightenment contained in the Areal was available to slaves in the North and South, Walker saw to it that the Pamphlet reached slaves in the Deep South also. The Pamphlet was smuggled onto ships heading for southern ports, secretly placed in cargo holds, and, loosely left in conspicuous places.

<u>Walker's Appeal</u> was radical in the sense of suggesting and advocating a more confronting and immediate attack on slavery. The confronting tone of the <u>Appeal</u> can be heard in its forceful and combative nature. Walker ventured that "anyone who would not fight for freedom should be kept in perpetual slavery, along with his children forever." Vincent Harding is quite perceptive in his understanding that Walker saw the black struggle for freedom in the same light as the Crusaders had seen their struggle. He suggests that black resistance to slavery was tantamount to the obedience of God's will, while continued obedience to slavery was sinful and would warrant the eventual judgment of God on the black sinner. Walker was so committed to freedom and to preventing slavery from becoming a malady for blacks that he ventured to say, "I will stand my ground ... and somebody must die in the

---

[123] Ibid., p. 88.

cause." This self-fulfilling prophecy was realized on June 28, 1830, at the door of his shop in Boston where he was found dead. The true cause of his death was and, still is uncertain. However, most evidence points to poisoning, but Donald M. Jacobs disagrees with that conclusion. He is of the opinion that his death was due to natural causes. Jacobs also raises questions about Walker's age upon his death; relying on the report of Henry Highland Garnet, who is the first writer to give the date of Walker's birth, who states that Walker's death, occurred at age thirty-four. Garnet does not indicate foul play or the possibility of murder; rather, he mentions that Walker died in "1831 in Bridge Street, at the hopeful and enthusiastic age of 44 years." The historical discrepancies suggest that the book on Walker's like has not fully been closed.

It seems safe to posit that Walker's Appeal was one of the most revolutionary and anarchistic pieces of literary propaganda to appear on the American scene during the turn of the nineteenth century. However, it was not the only controversial material to appear during that era of American History. During the same time that Walker's Appeal appeared, Robert Young shocked the Nation with the publication of what was called The Ethiopian Manifesto, which attempted to further express and explain the specifics of the thoughts contained in the Appeal.[124] The Ethiopian Manifesto picked up on the

---

[124] Donald M. Jacobs. "David Walker, Boston Race Leader, 1825-1830", (Essex Institute Historical Collections, January 1971), pp. 94-107

ideas contained in the <u>Appeal</u> and pushed them forward. Young was in touch with the thoughts of those black leaders of the nineteenth century whose primary bases for actions were the Holy Bible as they understood it. Therefore, in that sense, the word Ethiopia was another word for Africa, the land from which the slaves had been transported and forced to live a slave existence in America. Walker seemed to advocate a degree of social and political co-existence between the races, while Young seemed to suggest the establishment of Ethiopian people here in America. Theocracy is a government in which God is the supreme ruler. Young articulates these theocratic ideas when he says:

> "Beholding but one sole power, supremacy, or head, we do if that head ... look forward for succor in the accomplishment of the great design, which he hath, in his wisdom, prompted us to its undertakings. Inherent within the Manifesto is the immediate arrival of liberation for the slaves. The Ethiopian Manifesto is an announcement to the black people of America that the time of freedom has come."

Here Young alludes to a divine-human enterprise, and when, "... with the power of words, and the divine will of our God, the vile shackles of slavery shall be broken asunder from you, and no man known shall dare to claim or proclaim man as his bondsman." Young, as Walker had done before him, pointed black America to immediate freedom. However, there seems to be a different understanding as to the process of the ultimate realization of the liberation to which Young referred. While Walker perceives that freedom is imminent, but it will necessitate the death of someone, Young seems to feel that freedom will come through the words of man and the power of God.

Walker is clear as to the potential of death as a sacrifice for the eventual liberation of the slaves, "Somebody must die in this cause. I may be doomed to the stake and the fire, or to the scaffold tree, but it is not in me to falter if I can promote the work of emancipation."

The Appeal was considered so radical that it aroused the anger of both slave owners and some disagreement from abolitionists. Herbert Aptheker states that the level of anger and hostility toward the writer of the Appeal was such that the bounty was eventually raised to $300.[125] Leon F. Litwack points to Robert Alexander Young's, The Ethiopian Manifesto, (New York, 1829), in which he noted that William Floyd Garrison had recently launched his anti-slaves crusade as editor of The Liberator, and had expressed some strong disagreements with the general tone and the "general spirit of Walker's Appeal, but Garrison later admitted that "many valuable truths and warnings were contained therein." Litwack does not end his presentation on pro-abolitionists' anti-Appeal sentiments, and neither does he suggest that the South

---

[125] Sterling Stuckey. The Ideological Origins of Black Nationalism. (Boston: Beacon Press, 1972), pp. 32-34.

was the only region opposed to the The appearance of the Appeal and the contents contained therein. Litwack also reports the Northern negative sentiments towards the contents of the Appeal. The resolution of and approach to healing America's slave ills, as perceived by Walker, was too radical for anti-slavery advocate Benjamin Lundy, who later declared, "I can do no less than set the broadest seal of condemnation on it." Thus, the white forces in the liberation struggle for blacks share the social and political beliefs that blacks ought to be free, but could not agree with the tone and radical resistance nature of Walker's Appeal. This is both understandable and deplorable. It is understandable because one has to live the experience from within to fully grasp the internal horrors and turmoil felt by the slave. One who lives the experience knows the pain and suffering personally, while one who gets in touch with the pain through a second-hand source tends to react second-handed. While their commitment is nonetheless genuine and authentic; however, the immediacy and dire straits of the situation and the means and methods of delivery are essentially different. James Cone states that "Truth cannot be separated from the people's struggle and the hopes and dreams that arise from the struggle is... that transcendent reality, that is disclosed in peoples' historical desires and struggles for liberation." While the white forces involved In the liberation struggles were invaluable to the historical struggle for black liberation, whites can never feel the same degree of pain felt and experienced by the slave. Thus, Lundy and Garrison are considerably understood in their condemnation of Walker.

The contents and tone of the <u>Appeal</u> challenged and threatened the slave system in America in that it sets forth four basic reasons for the plight and wretchedness of the slaves.[126] The first reason is caused by slavery itself; the second is caused by ignorance, the third is caused by the preachers of the Christian religion and, the fourth is caused by the Colonization Movement. This chapter examines the four basic conditions associated with the system which Walker posited as contributing to a national ill, called slavery. This chapter examines the four articles of the <u>Appeal</u> and ascertains what Walker's concept of freedom and liberation is contained therein. The primary focus of this chapter is to focus on freedom and liberation as they are words. The two words are used interchangeably to accentuate the depths and scope of what freedom and liberation meant for Walker, translated into the lives of the slaves. While both words are used, for Walker, the word freedom is more frequently used. But the word freedom suggests intangibles, while the word liberation suggests something with which we are most familiar and it has more tangibility for this study than does the word freedom. The word freedom suggests a price to be paid to make something a reality, liberation suggests release, or the unhindered right to do and to be without having a monetary, political, and social decision attached.

---

[126] Leon F. Litwack. <u>North of Slavery</u>. (Chicago: The University of Chicago Press,1961), pp. 191.

Therefore, there is the doing and being without having to base the right to do and be on any human being's decisions or mandates, rather they are based on the fact of being alive and a part of human creation. It is in that sense that the word liberation is used within the context of this study. In order to better understand Walker's concept of freedom; each of the four articles is examined to set forth Walker's understanding of the slaves' political, social, and religious predicaments. After examining each article, there follows what is his understanding of freedom and liberation. In the first article, Walker posits that the wretchedness of the slave is caused by the slave system itself.

"OUR WRETCHEDNESS CAUSED BY SLAVERY"

Herbert Aptheker, in his "One Continual Cry" the main reason for the long delay in a total black revolution rest in the fact that the actuality and depths of the black plight were not fully understood in all parts of the confederacy; if so, one continual cry would be raised in all parts of the confederacy and would cease only with the complete overthrow of the system of slavery in every part of the country. Aptheker posits that slavery was a form of tyranny that maintained a system of control over a segment of society. He further posits that that segment represented the labor force that ensured the economic wealth and status of the ruling class. Karl Marx's position that slavery was "a commercial system of exploitation: captures the essence of what slavery was all about. It was from free slave labor that came the rice, sugar, cotton, coal, lumber, and gold that represented billions of dollars for the master while never building any cash value to the slave's account. Instead, the coffers of the capitalistic system of the United States draw by the billions while the slave remained a slave. Aptheker further asserts that to maintain a capitalistic system of growth for the powerful, "there were no limits imposed on the exploitations of slave owners." It is difficult to understand the nature and depths of <u>Walker's Appeal</u> without having an understanding of the system of slavery itself. The <u>Appeal</u> was not an isolated, disjointed, and foreign document; it emerged from a situation that was real for the slaves and for all readers, North and South. A number of Americans who sat in seats of influence and authority insisted that slavery was neither a bad nor an inhumane system, while others insisted that slavery was ordained in the Bible. Aptheker cites a famous sermon delivered by the Reverend William Meade, who served as Bishop in the Episcopal Church in Virginia, and was also a leader in 1816-1817, who assured the slaves that "God has willed that they occupy their lowly position ... if not. they will suffer eternally in Hell." The extent to which religious prostitution contributed to the slaves' wretchedness is discussed later; however, such teachings were a part of a larger scheme concocted by slave owners mid their preachers to perpetuate an evil system.

David Walker joined the list of petitioners in the struggle for freedom who were of the obsession that the written word is a potent force in the liberation crusade.

Walker assumes that slavery was known to exist in human history, but that the severity of the suffering and the dehumanization that resulted would render the economic, social, and political gains associated with and derived from it negatively; negative in the sense that no level of growth and economic wealth is worth the dehumanization of one single individual. Martin Buber is accurately perceptive in his "I-Thou" relationships and his "I-IT" relationships. What Buber has in mind is that things are less important than persons. Therefore, persons are ends within themselves rather than means to ends. Walker saw slavery as an "I-lT" system that utilized a person for the sole purpose of realizing an individual end.[127] This perception of slavery, as Walker understood it, places man in a position of utter wretchedness by rendering himself less than a total person. To articulate the wretchedness of the slave, Walker publishes his Appeal, and has it distributed in many parts of America. The question comes to mind, what is the power of the pen?" As it is coupled with the spoken word, America was in for a rude awakening! For many years there had been efforts made on the part of blacks to present to the public eye the plight of the slave.

This had been done through petitions, one such petition was sent from Philadelphia, Pennsylvania in 1800 by the Reverend Absalom Jones calling on Congress to enact legislation preventing the African slave trade.

---

[127] Herbert Aptheker. One Continual Cry: David Walker's Appeal to the Colored Citizens of the World. (New York: Humanities Press, 1965), pp. 8-10.

But the traditional response to petitions sent by blacks, it was to refer them to committees to ensure a sudden death; the Jones' petition was also to experience sudden death. However, the Appeal was written with such accuracy of facts, the force of the pen, and saturated with such Christian principles and ideals that it was assured to get the attention of its readers, thus avoiding sudden death.

Walker felt that the power of the pen was an effective avenue of approach to informing America in general and the slave particularly, of the horrors of slavery in Walker's "One Continual Cry." This suggests that America has not reacted to slavery in a more positive way simply because America has not been informed as to the realities of the slave system. Therefore, the Appeal is to inform America, hoping to elicit an immediate reaction from all parts of the country that would reflect a Continual Cry for slave freedom and liberation.

Walker realized the limited communication systems of the nineteenth century that were open to the slaves, and the constraints placed on Negro education, word-of-mouth was to be used as the slave's basic communication method. Communication was also done through songs and signs; much of this was communicated during social gatherings between plantation slaves, domestic servants, at religious worship. James Cone has adequately validated the role and function of the song in the Black religious' experience. The song was an effective means of communicating the inherent desires for freedom and, the means of escape. The songs of the slaves had housed within them buzz words, signs, and symbols, and were the rallying cries for freedom. One such song which simultaneously predicted the ultimate destruction of the slave owner and his system and, the freedom of the slave is poetically captured in the famous song: "Oh Mary, don't weep, don't you moan, Pharaoh's Army got drowned, Oh Mary, don't you weep." The only one that is oblivious to Biblical history would fail to understand the message of the song. Historically, the song's theme is seen in the Biblical Account of Pharaoh's Army of ancient Egypt being destroyed as they tried to delay and prevent the Israelites from achieving their liberation from Egyptian bondage. The slave, with limited literary' exposure, was able to perceive a close parallel between the events in Israel's liberation and those in the Black liberation struggles in America. For the Black slaves, freedom and liberation was a single movement in their historical existence. Therefore, based on historical precedents, the slaves found hope for their liberation and they communicated these ambitious hopes and dreams to other slaves through the power of the pen, as is seen in the <u>Appeal</u> and through songs such as the one quoted above. With the historical and Biblical precedents of slave liberation and the songs of the Black experiences, Walker was quite familiar and, understood fully the intentions of the symbolism and messages of the songs. But he saw them as no substitute for the power of the pen. As one involved in the Methodist Church in Boston, Massachusetts, he would have even sung songs of liberation, but the songs of liberation were songs that needed corresponding verbal treatise which led to immediate actions which would result in the total liberation of the slaves all across America. Thus, Walker employs the power of the written word that ultimately transcended, in terms of scope, the community of the slave and extended to the larger communities of economics and politics.

The <u>Appeal</u> was successful in reaching those arenas through unorthodox means of smuggling them onto shops headed for southern ports, to the inconspicuous plantings of them in clothing to be sold to sailors. The identity of Blacks had been well established by whites by the nineteenth century. From the advent of slave trading by Europeans, the worth and value of African people lead been determined and laws were now enacted to enforce the nature, role, and self-worth of each slave. The laws enacted to control a species of property were arbitrary and bent toward the advantage of whites. Thus those of the planter's class and those given to commercial exploitation and leadership in the South were virtually free to bring in unlimited numbers of slaves to increase the slave owner's wealth and productivity, and the resulting profits. Should the attitudes and efforts of resistance develop among the slaves, there were always available to the master the whips, the guns, the laws, and the scaffolds of punishments? These methods of depression, suppression, and oppression were effectively employed by the slave masters, but <u>Walker's Appeal</u> pointed out the horrors of slavery and liberation from the fears of physical, mental, and political oppression.[128] Donald M. Jacobs is accurate in his perception of southern reaction to the <u>Appeal</u> as being an incitement to insurrection among Blacks. In the <u>Appeal</u>, Walker raises what is for him, a rhetorical question of the true identity of the slave: "Are we men!! I ask you, oh my brethren! Are we women?" For Walker, the answer was a resounding Yes! but while he was convinced as to the true identity of the slave, there were millions of fellow blacks in the North and in the South who had fallen under the curse of a slave mentality. Walker is very much aware of the mentality forced upon many slaves by the slave system. He cites incidents in which blacks sold fellow blacks into slavery for "the paltry sum of $50, or expose the places in which runaway slaves were hiding for a glass of whiskey.'" The <u>Appeal</u> sets out to facilitate in the mind of the slave a true sense of identity and to four a spirit and sense of self-worth, dignity, collegiality, and cooperation among them that he felt would assist in ultimately actualizing their liberation. Walker is mindful of the lack of unity, goal, and purpose that permeates the black community of all blacks regardless of their geographical locations in America; thus he anticipated opposition from within his own ethnic community; from persons whom he describes as being "ignorantly in league with slaveholders." He identifies them as those who get "their daily bread by the blood and sweat

---

[128] Donald M. Jacobs. "David Walker: Boston Race header. 1825-1830". (Essex Institute Historical Collections. January 1971), pp. 94-107.

of their more ignorant brethren." and as persons who cannot see beyond their noses," but will rise against him for his efforts of liberation and call him cursed. Walker is here hitting at a major deterrent and an impediment to liberation, a divided black community. Donald M. Jacobs is again perceptive in his assessment of Walker's motive for pushing for Black unity and solidarity. Jacobs cites an article in the 1824 issue of the Boston Columbian Sentinel in which Walker applauds a number of whites who joined blacks in championing the cause of liberation at the expense of paying the ultimate price, death. Walker's real motive is to point out to fellow blacks that while white men give their lives and sacrifice their futures in the cause of black liberation, he could not allow blacks to become complacent and less involved than whites in the black liberation struggle. Walker had in mind those whites, such as Colonel Jonathan Granville who had been involved in the Haitian Colonization plan, Benjamin Lundy who also supported the Haitian scheme, and Vehudi Ashmun who was a former Colonial agent for Liberia whom Walker referred to as having "lost his life for our cause."[129] The American slave institution with its consequences of wretchedness motivated Walker to engage in literary exposure that would appraise America of the wretchedness of slavery at a level that had not been exposed before. For some reason, Walker maintained his faith in a sense of moral justice which he felt was held by a large segment of the American society.

---

[129] Donald M. Jacobs, "David Walker's Appeal", (Boston: Columbian Sentinel, 1824), pp. 8-10.

The thesis was that while slavery is seen as acceptable and proper by a significant segment of Americans, his belief was that there were many Americans who were not pro-slavery. Walker's expressed presupposition, which is inherent in the opening sentences of the Appeal, is that the reason why slavery is tolerated in America is that the majority of Americans are not aware of the wretchedness of slavery. Walker knew quite well that the liberation initiative would not emerge from the slave holders' pen; rather it must emerge from the pen of one who, while not a slave himself, could identify with the slave's dilemma. It was this kind of mentality possessed by an ex-slave, Anthony Burns, who said that "God made me a man, not a slave, and gave me the same right to myself that he gave to the man who stole me to himself." Throughout <u>Walker's Appeal</u> is the theme of self-liberation in which he urged blacks to become actively involved in the process of freedom. He held before the slave the idea and fact that liberation must first come from within his own psyche and then reveal itself in creative and productive corresponding actions. This is why he raises the question: "Should the tyrants take it into their heads to emancipate any of you, remember that your freedom is your natural right ... if they do not want to part with your labor ... God Almighty will break their strong band. The wretchedness of the slave caused by slavery is set forth in Article I of the Appeal and, it seeks to point out to the readers the true horrors of slavery and, the mental state in which the slave must reach before freedom and liberation become a reality.[130] "The slave must experience internal freedom which makes him accept himself as a total person equal to any person and this internal affirmation of equal self-worth will reveal itself in external actions of liberation." This is why Walker attested that his only motivation for writing the <u>Appeal</u> was "to awaken in the breasts of my attainted, degraded and slumbering brethren, a spirit of inquiry and investigation respecting our miseries and wretchedness ..."[131]

Wretchedness has rendered the slave an object of degradation, dehumanization, and a non-person. What Walker does in the <u>Appeal</u> is draw upon traditional African approaches by which he would expose Americans to the questions relating to the reality of slavery. The first question is related to the reasons for black oppression, and the second is to speak the truth of both the oppressed and the oppressor in order to expose the contradictions between slavery and the American Dream for all Americans. The core of Walker's exposures were set forth in the ten major themes which point out the degradation of African people, nine are listed below: (1) the unavoidable judgment that a just God would bring upon white Americans, (2) the imperative for blacks to resist their oppressions, (3) the need for black solidarity, (4) his opposition to Colonization, (5)

---

[130] Carter G. Woodson. A Letter of Anthony Burns to the Baptist Church at Union Fauquier County Virginia" The Mind of the Negro as Reflected in Letters written during The Crisis. (New York: Arno Press, 1969), p. 163.

[131] David Walker and Henry Highland Garnet. <u>Walker's Appeal and Garnet's Address</u>. (New York: Arno Press, 1969), pp. 43-44.

the need for black education, (6) the possibility of a new society emerging out of a change of white attitudes toward blacks, (7) the need for Protestant Christian Religion to underbid the black struggle for freedom, (8) the prediction of his own death or imprisonment and, (9) his own sense of solidarity with his enslaved brothers and sisters. Walker's ten-step exposure implicated white Americans as racists who suppress and oppress blacks in order to advance their own cause and, he points out the obvious contradictions between the Declaration of Independence and the actual plight of blacks in America. The general intent of the Appeal is to lay before America the shamefulness of slavery hoping to provoke an immediate positive anti-slavery response front both the slave and those white Americans who also detested slavery. Walker's goal was accomplished to some degree among blacks because for nearly a century following his death, in 1834, his Appeal was still seen as a sourcebook for black solidarity and as solid as mason's for resisting slavery. The success of the Appeal, as Vincent Harding suggests, lay in "the breadth and honesty of its analysis,

... of its commitment to black liberations."[132] Article I of the Appeal is also designed to force white Americans to take another look at another aspect of human reality. This aspect of reality reveals the existential situation of the person who lived out his life as a non-person in the United States of America. Walker was aware of the fact

---

[132] Vincent Harding. There Is A River: The Black Struggle for Freedom in America. (New York: Harcourt Brace Jovanovich, 1981), pp. 3-5.

that in order for a person to break out of their cultural and politically self-imposed boxes of life and encounter another reality, they must be challenged to take seriously another look at other value systems and ways of life. Walker challenges his readers to not only commit themselves to Thomas Jefferson and Henry Clay, but also to take a look at the message and challenges of the Appeal. Walker understood well, and gave his readers the same credit for the same level of intelligence, that truth is relative based upon the level that available truth reflects. His inherent belief was that if more truth were revealed, then the white and black responses would be different and more positive toward the liberation of the slave. Walker posits that the reality of the wretchedness of the slave has direct consequences of slavery and is a primary impediment to liberation.

Walker promises in the early sentences of his Appeal to "demonstrate to the satisfaction of the most incredulous, that we colored people of these United States of America are the most wretched, degraded, and abject set of beings that ever lived since the world began." He does this by firstly appealing to those whom he calls "an enlightened and Christian people." By appealing to what he calls the Christian consciousness of the slaveholder, he raises the moral and ethical questions of ought, rightness, and wrongness. Walker resorted to the approach of moral suasion hoping to win on the basis of consciousness. He lays before the American public those who had access to and would read the Appeal in general and before the slaveholders specifically what he perceived as the core ills of America as they relate to the slave: "slavery, ignorance, religious preaching of the slave preachers and, Colonization in Africa," Slavery, for Walker, was commercial exploitation fueled by racism and the degrading of persons based solely upon the self- informed opinion of the inferiority of the slave. Walker lays in view of the historical accounts of preceding national powers of the past: Egyptians and their treatment of the Israelites under Pharaoh; the Helots among the Spartans, and the Greeks among the Turks, slavery, and slavery in ancient Rome. The term wretchedness seems to capture and express for Walker the plight of the slave's" day-to-day existence.

For Walker wretchedness is also a theological term that depicts the lowest level of the sinner's existence, from which only God can deliver. While Walker sees the possibility of the slave's liberation being actualized by the slave master, he realizes the remoteness of such reality. Therefore, there has to be a divine intervention on the part of man to ensure the liberation for which Walker was struggling. Herbert Aptheker cites the testimony of an Army Major, Amos Stoddard, who had served in Louisiana as far back as 1811. Major

A. Stoddard asserts that "cruel and even unusual punishment is daily inflicted on these wretched creatures, enfeebled, oppressed with hunger, labor and lash."[133] The Major's testimony is further helpful in understanding the horrors of the slave system as he describes the actual scenes of slave existence,

---

[133] Herbert Aptheker. <u>One Continual Cry</u>. (New York: Humanities Press, 1965), pp. 3-5.

he continued: "The scenes of misery and distress constantly witnessed along the coast of the Delta, the wounds and lacerations occasioned by demoralized masters and overseers, most of whom exhibit a strange compound of ignorance and depravity that torture the feelings of the passing stranger, and wring blood from his heart. Good, God! Why sleep thy vengeance!" It is well established historically that slavery was and is an inhumane system regardless of the society and culture in which it is practiced; and Walker was aware of this reality, he is also aware that slavery in the United States was allowed to reach, or descend to the lowest levels of depravity known to civilized man. Major Stoddard, obviously a white man based on his military rank, even found it difficult to understand and tolerate such treatments of fellow human beings and engages in questioning God for allowing the slave to endure the harshness of slavery. Stoddard uses the word wretched to describe the plight of the slave, as does Walker in later years. While, apparently, Walker was not familiar with Stoddard's writings, he was familiar with the day-to-day wretchedness of the slave. That is why he posits that "Our Wretchedness" is the consequence of slavery. Frequently, these words and symbols emerge out of the reader's own experiences in order to better communicate to the reader the true impact and thrust of the message. Rudolph Bultmann, a noted German New Testament theologian, says that language about God is mythological. Mythological in the sense that it is earth's language used by humans to express knowledge about one who is above the level of human existence.

Paul Tillich, a noted Philosopher-theologian, posits that theology is culturological, meaning that it is God expressed in terms of language and culture that makes it relevant to the culture it seeks to address. The terms wretched and wretch were used within the Christian religious confines to express the level of degradation to which God's human creature had fallen. The line in the famous hymn, "Amazing Grace! How Sweet the Sound, That saved a wretch like we!" written by John Newton, a former slave ship Captain who lived from 1720-1807, was perhaps very familiar to Walker and too many of the slaves. 'Wretch" conveys the idea and reality of the level of existence to which Newton confesses that he had fallen and, that only God could rescue and liberate him. It was in the sense of the slaves' wretchedness that Walker appealed to "heaven and earth, and particularly to the American people themselves, who cease not to declare that our condition is not hard," and that the slave is satisfied to "rest in wretchedness and misery." The majority of the slaves, while submitting to slaves at the surface level, never fully accepted the theory of their subhuman nature nor that God predestined them for slavery. James Cone has rightly perceived and posited that black theology is in, and emerges out of the experiences of black people and their understanding of the Holy Bible, especially the Exodus story.

Thus, freedom and liberation from the wretchedness caused by slavery were always an irrepressible desire of the slave. To express the horrors of slavery and the desire to be liberated, this song or poetic words were written: "O Freedom, O Freedom, O Freedom over me! Before I'll be a slave I'll be buried in my grave and go home to my Lord and be free." For Walker, the wretchedness of the slave was a state into which slavery had placed him and not a divine decree to be executed by the slave master.

There has been a discussion, and positions are taken, within black theological circles that tended to focus on black religion as primarily otherworldly and compensatory. Benjamin Elijah Mays and Joseph Nicholson advance this thesis in their book, The Negro Church. The thesis advances the idea that black religion was so preoccupied with the hereafter that the existential aspects of life here on earth were of secondary importance.[134] However, Mays and Nicholson point out that this idea was most prominent among those who fared worst in this world, with the Negro, it could hardly have been otherwise. His 244 years of slavery and the continuous prescription inflicted upon him since his emancipation has been all conducive to developing an other-worldly view in which the righteousness of God would be vindicated and his suffering people delivered. Seeing little or no hope in this world, "The Negro has done what other people have done, he has projected his hopes in heaven above."

Five years later, in 1938, Mays published another book entitled, The Negro's God, in which he maintained the same basic belief, although he made an exception

---

[134] Cecil Wayne Cone. The Identity Crisis in Black Theology. (Nashville: African Methodist Episcopal Church Press, 1975), pp. 58-59.

that some blacks understood the significance of this world while the masses of blacks viewed religion in an other-worldly sense; Mays arrives at this conclusion based upon black sermons, prayers, and black literature. A number of blacks held on to this until the mid-sixties when a, closer look was given to the nature and content of black preaching and songs. The "O Freedom" song as seen above suggests the desire for freedom here on earth, but if that freedom does not become a reality here, "Before I'll be a slave, I'll be buried in my grave." One has to admit that while a number of blacks posited their hopes in the world to come, it was done out of frustration and not out of denial of the reality of this world. The wretchedness of the slave brought on by the slave system placed the slave in an oppressive and inhuman condition, from which Walker sought relief. The question to be asked is how did Walker ascertain his insights into the conditions of the slave that led him to conclude that they were wretched? Walker was not a slave himself, however, he was able to travel through a number of areas in the United States and observe firsthand the conditions about which he would write later. While traveling through the North and South he made mental and written notes of his observations and, based upon them he concluded that "black Americans were the most wretched, degraded, and abject of people since the world began."[135] The wretchedness of the slave to which Walker refers is the direct consequence of slavery. Therefore, the cure to or the road to curing

---

[135] Ibid., pp. 22-23.

and riding blacks of the wretchedness that the slave experience brings, slavery must be forever eradicated from the black reality. Walker contrasts slavery in America to slavery practiced in the ancient world; Egypt, Greece, and Rome. He points out the treatment of Joseph in Egypt, who was an Israelite slave there, who was allowed to rise to a level of prominence in the palace of Pharaoh? Walker raises the question and challenges his fellow blacks to show him a black President, a Governor, a legislator, a Senator, a Mayor, or an Attorney of the Bar. He even challenges his fellow blacks to show him a person of coltur color) (sic) who holds the low office of Constable, or black men who sit on a Jury. Walker concludes that while Egypt predates the Christian Era, the Egyptians were more civilized than Christian America in a sense because of the treatment of their slaves. Walker is here emphasizing what he perceives as the true effect that Christianity should have on one's life and behavior. With the benefits of Christianity, one is expected to both understand and accept all members of God's human creation as equals. Walker launches some of his most severe criticism of American slavery because America professed to be a Christian nation. The wretchedness of the slaves perpetuated upon them by a Christian nation was the worst form of hypocrisy.

Thus, Walker is critical of America's inconsistency of theory and practice regarding the slave issue. But in spite of his criticism of America's brand of Christianity, Walker remained loyal to what he saw as biblical Christianity and, with that faith in the Bible and in God, he held on to the belief in the ultimate redemption of

America. In spite of the wretchedness of the slave, Walker maintained that "blacks should continue their fight for liberation here in America rather than become pessimistic and resort to Africa and Colonization for help." At this point, Walker reflects on the influence of Richard Allen, a Bishop in the African Methodist Episcopal Church, took a strong position against Colonization in Africa.

Throughout the first Article within the Appeal, Walker argues that there is an inextricable link between the condition of the slave and that of the slave system. The slave system rendered black slaves less than a whole person and, commenced to treat them accordingly.[136] The principles and practices of slavery in America are well documented, verified, and validated historically. Walker acknowledges slavery as an economic and political reality in America, but unlike those who profited from the economic wealth of slavery, he envisioned a day of liberation for all the slaves in America. One aspect and reality of liberation for Walker was land ownership. Because Walker emerges out of a religious background, he frequently understands history in light of Biblical history in general and, the history of the Israelites specifically. Out of this sense of Biblical History, Walker develops a theology of liberation. Liberation for Walker involves land ownership as was seen in the history of Israel in Egypt. He cites that while in Egypt, the Israelites were given the land of Goshen in

---

[136] Sterling Stuckey. Walker's Appeal: The Ideological Origins of Black Nationalism. (Boston: Beacon Press, 1972), pp. 80-82.

which to live. It is significant for Walker that a nation, which he saw as being led by "heathen Pharaoh," compared with ours under the "enlightened Christians of America" as being more humane, benevolent, and less violent than a nation that identifies with Christianity. Walker raises the question of land ownership and asks the rhetorical question: "Where is the most barren spot of land which they have given us?" Not only were the slaves not given land, but Walker also cites a situation in which a black man had "labored (sic) day and night to acquire a little money, and having acquired it, he vested it in a small piece of land, and got him a house erected thereon, and having paid for the whole, ... was cheated out of his property by a white man, driven out of his land!" Land ownership for Walker provided a sense of liberation and was a symbol of progress, stability, and self-worth. Therefore, freedom and liberation were not limited to the movement of the physical body but were the freedom to act out those internal desires and feelings to the extent to which the person realizes equal worth and experienced the full benefits of dignity.

Walker was disturbed at the manner in which white Americans perceived black Americans. He alludes to the Israelite's tenure in Egypt, slaves they were, and points out that they were never dehumanized to the point of suggesting that they were beings who were descendants of "Monkeys or Orangutans," and not humans. Walker is perceptive as he emphasizes the fact that instead of the Pharaoh perceiving the Israelites as the descendants of monkeys, they were treated as fellow human beings and allowed to reach levels of social and political prominence. He cites Joseph as an influence in Pharaoh's court and Moses as being adopted by the daughter of Pharaoh and later raised to the level of Prince Regent to the throne of Egypt.[137] The humane and respectful treatment of the Israelite slaves in Egypt is placed alongside the inhumane treatment of the black slaves in America by the slave system and, out of this dynamic Walker sees where slavery in America has rendered, wretchedness upon blacks, which stands in the way of real freedom of man's liberation. It is obvious that the subhuman tactic used by the slave master was designed to convince the slave that he was less than a person, thus any idea of orienting the slave for those positions of power, influence, and educational development was beyond his grasp. To further promote a complex of inferiority among slaves, there were instituted slave codes that completely deprived black people of their inherent rights as human beings. Their labor and their lives were under the constant supervision and critical eye of the mastery of the owners. This mastery of ownership extended to every aspect of the slave's life: marriage, property ownership, and human personality were denied. The history of the prohibitory statute tells only parts of the day-to-day meager existence of the slave, for the more oppressive still was the private tyranny and the absolute control of the masters, sanctioned by the law as the only effective means of policing the unwilling and rebellious labor force.

---

[137] Holy Bible, Genesis 47: 5-6.

CHAPTER VIII
CONCLUSION

The most difficult and incomprehensible chapter in the history of the United States of America is the chapter in which the history of American slavery is recorded. Slavery in the United States represents a relatively long period in American History, (or in the history of America because the extent of brutality perpetrated upon the slave is not essentially recorded in the annals of American History) which subjugated people of color to a degree of servitude that is unparalleled in the history of human relationships. Slavery as was experienced by Blacks in the United States of America was unique in the sense that it was predicated upon the social and biological presupposition that blackness was inherently inferior to whiteness. This presupposition is evident in all of the social, economic, cultural, political, and religious relationships between White Americans and Black Americans. Carl N. Degler has raised the crucial question, whether rhetorical or inquisitive, as to the causes of race prejudice. The question was and seems to remain, "Did race prejudice cause slavery, or did slavery cause race prejudice?" Degler posits that slavery was based on the assumption that blacks were biologically inferior to whites and, therefore blacks were natural slaves.[138]

The history of the United States is a living reminder that here once lived a people whose skin color was/is different from that of whites and that people were subjected to a degree of bondage unlike any other people of the civilized world. Not only is there a history of that experience, but also there is a long history of human efforts to rid the Nation of the perpetuation of slavery in the United States.

This is a history that began even before Blacks were bought/stolen on the shores of Africa and transported to the "New World," and placed in involuntary servitude for several centuries. The insatiable motivation for slave revolts, or efforts to win freedom, was to liberate themselves from social conditions that deprived them of the opportunity to express themselves as total human beings.

Slavery was always ironic to the expressed goals and words of the Declaration of Independence and the Constitution of the United States. If irony means the "opposite of what might be expected," then the magnificent words of the Declaration of Independence are ironic, indeed. Ironic in the sense that Dr. Johnson, the English Tory, noted when he expresses: "How is it

---

[138] An Essay by Carl N. Degler "The Irony of American Negro Slavery" in <u>Perspectives and Irony in American History</u>, ed. By Harry P. Owens. (Jackson, Mississippi: The University of Mississippi Press, 1976), pp. 12-15.

that we hear the loudest yelps for liberty among the drivers of Negroes?"

The American society allowed itself to develop during the early stages of its history an institution that was to be known later as a lucrative system of chattel slavery. This system later became an American nightmare that affected nearly every aspect of American life and thought. From the remotest cotton patches of the rural South to the industrialized section the Northern corridors of the Nation were there known and experienced the perils of the slave system. While the Northern states' levels of participation in the slave system were, somewhat, less than that of the Southern states, the impact was realized and experienced by people in both North and South. One is safe to posit that the system would have prevailed much longer had it not been for men and women who detested the slave system and gave of their lives, their personal and social fortunes, and their political and economic security to protest a system they held as evil and, which ran counter to what the United States of America was all about. American slavery was an irony! American slavery poised itself as a step toward civilization! American slavery was held by a number of its supporters as a school of learning! However, schools and learning suggest growth and eventual graduation date, neither of which was a reality in the slave system.

David Walker and the positions taken in his Appeal is an early American voice that sought to call to the attention of America the levels of degradation to which slavery lowered a person. David Walker's Appeal of 1829 was an attention-getter, to say the least. It was among the first pieces of anti-slavery literature to surface in the United States of America that was well written and stirred up the consciousness of America. Many scholars, including Herbert Aptheker, Eugene Genevese, John W. Blassingame, Albert J. Rebateau, and Melville Herskovitz have thoroughly researched the slave era in the United States of America, each of whom has pointed up that slavery was a horrible and inhumane system that stands as America's darkest chapter in her history.

One of the foremost and dedicated disciples of David Walker was Henry Highland Garnet. Garnet was born on December 23, 1815, during the time when America was at one of its high points in the slave trade. Garnet was born in New Market Maryland, in Kent County. Significantly enough, Garnet's family was able to remain intact during those difficult times of slavery and he was able to develop within a family structure while many sons and daughters were being sold as slaves and transported to far-away plantations. Garnet's grandfather was a prince of the Mandingo Empire in West Africa before his slavery in America. This obvious contribution to the strong family ties later prepared Garnet for his involvement in the liberation struggles for slaves. In 1824, the Garnet family was able to escape from the Spencer plantation to Bucks County, Pennsylvania, and later to New York. Garnet was well educated for the times during which he lived: having attended the African Free School, The Presbyterian-affiliated Oneida Theological Institute, and his affiliation with the African Methodist Episcopal Church. From those launching pads, Garnet would become a staunch advocate of freedom.[139]

One of the most critical moments in Garnet's life occurred during the summer of 1846 when the "Colored American", a newspaper, called a convention. The purpose of the Convention was to solidify black political power. This convention set a precedent: it was the first time a convention was to be run by blacks. Henry Highland Garnet, Sam R. Ward, Crummell, and Theodore Wright were the main backers. This Convention was the initial effort on the part of Blacks to plan their own methods of liberation from slavery. By the mid-1840s, there were enough anti-slavery sentiments among blacks to mount a significant movement against slavery.

While whites had shown some interest in Black liberation, there was always present a sense among Blacks that white involvement was limited because it was being led by racism. This is seen in the addresses of Blacks where it was often pointed out by Blacks that "... it is easy to ask about the vileness of slavery in the South ... but to call the dark man a brother ... that is the test."[140] Perhaps that remains to be a test today as to whether one's involvement in the freedom struggle is equivalent to genuine authentic brotherhood or sisterhood. Henry Highland Garnet, and other Blacks, arrived at a point in their struggles for slave liberation at which the serious question of the true identity of Whites with Blacks

---

[139] Earl Ofari. Let Your Motto Be Resistance: The Life and Thought of Henry Highland Garnet. (Boston: Beacon Press. 1972), pp. 1-6.
[140] Ibid., p. 16.

during the liberation struggle. These questions were foundationally raised based on the history of Blacks not being a significant part of many abolitionist movements. Even among abolitionist movements whose "goal" was total liberation of the slaves, there were limited involvements on the part of Blacks. The Society for the Promoting of the abolition of Slavery, from 1775 to 1859 admitted only one black person, Robert Purvis.[141]141

Walker's Appeal had a tremendous impact on the life of Garnet. Beginning in 1843, Garnet expressed some of the influences of Walker during the Negro Convention held in New York. It was during this Convention that Garnet was to deliver his most powerful address, with radical orientations, entitled "An Address to the Slaves of the United States." The speech echoes Walker's thinking, coupled with Garnet's liberation fervor. The speech was reflective of Walker in tone and language: Freedom, Tyrants, Die, rather die freemen, than to live as slaves." Earl Ofari has captured, in his book entitled Let Your Motto Be Resistance: The Life and Thought of Henry Highland Garnet, the core of Henry Highland Garnet's life and thought as seen through his public speeches and lectures. Garnet represents the link between Walker and the liberation struggles of the 1860s, and even into the twentieth century.

While Henry Highland Garnet and many of his contemporaries blazed the trail for liberation; the final chapter remains to be written on the true abolition of slavery in the United States of America. Large numbers

---

[141] Ibid., p. 16.

of books have been written on the history of slavery as an institution in America, they all remain tentative rather than conclusions. The era that began in 1619 was not necessarily "conceived in liberty," nor was it "dedicated to the proposition that all men are created equal..." The history of America supports the fact that America's future development was predicated upon a slave and coerced labor force. From the advent of the arrival of twenty black indentured servants in Jamestown, Virginia in 1619 to the outbreak of the Revolutionary War in 1776, slavery spread throughout the English colonies like wildfires. The wildfires spread from Jamestown to every hamlet, wilderness, and village in America, and largely influenced the politics of both North and South for nearly three hundred years. Ultimately, it necessitated a Civil War, the 13th, 14th, and 15th Amendments to the United States Constitution to bring some sense of resolutions to the slave question.

An interesting chapter, "The End of Slavery", appears in Peter Kolchin's book, entitled <u>American Slavery: 1619-1877</u>, that talks about the military and political conflicts surrounding the Civil War, or the war to end Southern independence, as really a war about slavery. While the topic is stimulating, one must continually raise the question: Did slavery end after the Civil War? Or, was there a transition from one social status to another state, equally degrading? What were the differences between the black codes, Jim Crowism, Reconstruction, and racism during the period of segregation? These questions, the answers to which, remain the task of historians and social reformers.

In this study, I have traced the struggle for Black liberation from slavery in the United States of America from its inception, perhaps 1619, to the experiences and works of David Walker. I touched lightly on the life of Henry Highland Garnet, Nathaniel Paul, and the Rt. Reverend Richard Allen. Specific attention was given to <u>David Walker's Appeal</u> and to the immediate reactions voiced and the receptions of the <u>Appeal</u> in the North and in the South. From hostility to praises were typical responses to Walker's work, on the one hand, and the feelings of anarchy to disbelief on the other hand. Mayors and other politicians called for his arrest, and even abolitionists were in disagreement with his positions on the works of Walker. Nonetheless, the <u>Appeal</u> raised the level of consciousness of the American public, including the slaves. Herbert Aptheker is one of the most vociferous proponents of the position taken by Walker in the <u>Appeal</u>. In his book, <u>One Continual Cry</u>, Aptheker takes the position that if Americans only knew the depths and horrors of the slave systems, there would be made one continual cry for freedom. He suggests that the reason Americans have not come out against slavery more strongly is that they are unaware of its horrors and inequities, not to mention its degrading effects on the slaves.

    This study has sought to report the findings of credible scholarship to support the theses of Walker, which have been tentatively done and await further studies. True liberation in the United States must involve the freedom of all peoples who inhabit these lands, including all races, ethnic groups, religious orientations, political affiliations, gender, sexual preferences and cultural perspectives. One must not be discriminated against because of conditions experienced over which the individual has no control. Inherent within the ten's "liberation" is reconciliation. Reconciliation presupposes repentance that leads to forgiveness of sins, whether they be racial, political, economic, social, or religious sins. To comply with the mandates set forth in Walker's argument, the slaveholders' institution must offer some remorse: a change of heart, a change of mind, and, a change of direction that is evidence of true change that eventually translates into altered positive behavior.

<u>David Walker's Appeal to the Coloured Citizens of the World, But in Particular, and Very expressly, to Those of The United States of America</u>, written in 1829, was a clarion call that alerted America and the world as to the plight of Blacks in America. The life of Walker ended in a cloud of mystery however, his closest disciple, Henry Highland Garnet reported that he died in 1830 at the age "34 years (sic),"[142] which is impossible with a birth date of 1755. The 1820s until 1830 were considered the "Watershed" of the Black liberation struggles, which suggests that Walker was "a" Founding Father of civil rights and a pioneer of slave liberation in America. Comparable studies on the life and works of David Walker would contribute significantly to our ongoing understanding and appreciation of David Walker and of the struggles for freedom, the world over.

---

[142] Herbert Aptheker. One Continual Cry: David Walker's Appeal, Its Setting and Its Meaning. (New York: Humanities Press, 1965), p. 43.

BIBLIOGRAPHY

Adler, Mortimer J. We Hold These Truths. (New York: MacMillan Publishing, 1987), pp. 42-80.

Aptheker, Herbert. One Continual Cry: David Walker's Appeal to the Colored Citizens of the World. (New York: Humanities Press, 1965).

_____. Essays in the History of the American Negro. New York: International Publishers, 1964).

_____. To Be Free: Studies in American Negro History. (New York: International Publishers, 1969).

Bellagh, James Curtis. A History of Slavery in Virginia. (Baltimore, Maryland: Johns Hopkins University Press, 1902).

Barzun, Jacques and Graff, Henry F. The Modern Researchers. Rev. ed. (New York: Harcourt Brace, 1970).

Bedini, Silvo A. The Life of Benjamin Banneker. (New York: Charles Scribners' Sons, 1972).

Bennett, Lerone Jr, Before the Mayflower. (Chicago: Johnson Publishing Company, 1969).

Blassingame, John W. The Slave Community. (New York: Oxford University Press, 1979), pp. 128-134.

_____. Slave Testimony. (Baton Rouge, Louisiana: Louisiana State University Press, 1977).

Bruce, Henry Clay. The New Man: Twenty-Nine Years As A Slave, Twenty-Nine Years As A Free Man. (York, Pennsylvania: Anstadt Press, 1895), pp. 45-46

Carp, Robert A. and Stidham, Ronald. Judicial Process in America. (Washington, D. C.: Congressional Quarterly, 1990), pp. 26-27.

Cone, Cecil Wayne. The Identity Crisis in Black Theology. (Nashville, Tennessee: The African Methodist Episcopal Church Press, 1975).

Cone, James H. God of the Oppressed. (New York: The Seabury Press, 1975).

Carletone. Black Freedom. (London, England: The MacMillan Company, 1970).

Davidson, Basil. That African Slave Trade: Precolonial History: 1450-1850. (Atlantic Monthly Press Book, 1961), pp. 44-47.

David, Jay, ed. Black Defiance: Black Profiles in Courage. (New York: William Morrow & Company, 1972), pp. 1-2.

DeBow. "The Southern Cultivator", XX1. Vol. II. 1858.

Degler, Carl N. "Slavery and the Genesis of American Race Prejudice", in Comparative Studies in History and Society. II, (October, 1959).

DeBois. W.E.B. The Souls of Blacks. (Greenwich, Connecticut: Fawcett, 1961).

Elton, G. R. The Practice of History. (New York: Thomas Y. Crowell, 1967), p. 65.

_____. Suppression of the African Slave Trade to the United States of America: 1638-1870. (Cambridge: Russell and Russell, 1898).

Eaton Clement. The Freedom-of-thought Struggle in the Old South. (New York: Harper & Row Publishers, 1964).

_____. "A Dangerous Pamphlet in the Old South." Journal of Southern History, 1936.

Elkins, Stanley M. Slavery. (Chicago: The University of Chicago Press. 1968).

Federer, William J. Three Secular Reasons Why America Should be Under God. (St. Louis, MO. Amerisearch, Inc., 2008), p. 48.

Filler, Louis. The Crusade Against Slavery. (New York: Harper and Brothers, 1960).

Franklin, John Hope. From Slavery to Freedom. (New York: Vintage Books, 1969).

Frazier, E. Franklin. The Negro Church in America. (New York: Schocken Books, 1976).

Franklin, E. Frazier, and Lincoln, C. Eric. The Negro Church in America and the Black Church Since Frazier. (New York: Shocken Books, 1974).

Franklin, John Hope. From Slavery to Freedom: A History of Negro Americans. (New York: Random House, 1969), pp. 128-129, 138-139.

Frederickson, George M. The Black Image in the White Mind. (New York: Harper and Row Publishers, 1971).

"Freedom's Journal," November 2, 1827, Vol. I, No. 34.

_____. April 25, 1828. Vol. II, No. 5.

_____. December 19, 1828, Vol. II.

_____. October 24, 1829,

Garnet, Henry Highland. "Let Your Motto Be Resistance" in Sterling Stuckey's The Ideological Origins of Black Nationalism (Boston: Beacon Press, 1972).

Genovese, Eugene D. From Rebellion to Revolution. (Baton Rouge, Louisiana State University Press, 1979).

_____. Roll Jordan Roll. (New York: Pantheon Books. 1974).

George, Carol V. R. Segregated Sabbaths: Richard Allen and the Emergence of Independent Black Churches. (New York: Oxford University Press, 1973), pp. 21-23.

Good, Carter V. Essentials of Educational Research: Methodology and Design 2nd ed. (Englewood. Cliff, New Jersey: Prentice-Hall, 1972).

Gottschalk, Louis. Understanding History: A Primer of Historical Method. (New York: Alfred Knopf, 1961).

Harding, Vincent. There is a River: The Black Struggle for Freedom in America. (New York: Harcourt Brace Jovanovich, 1981).

The Holy Bible, Genesis 47: 5-6.

Jacobs, Donald M. "David Walker: Boston Race Leader, 1825-1830" (Essex Institute of Historical Collections, January, 1971)

Jefferson. Thomas. Notes on Virginia. (New York: Random House, 1944), p. 256.

Jones, Lawrence A. "They Sought A City: The Black Church and Churchmen in the Nineteenth-Century." Union Theological Seminary Quarterly Review, Spring, 1971).

Jordan, Winthrop D. White Over Black. (Chapel Hill, North Carolina: The University of North Carolina Press, 1968).

Katz, William Laren. Negro Protest Pamphlets. (New York: Arno Press and The New York Times, 1968).

King, Shaun. The New York Daily News. (November, 10, 2016, p.6

Lincoln, C. Eric. The Black Experience in Religion. (Garden City, New York: Anchor Press/Doubleday, 1974), pp. 10-11.

Litwack, Leon F. North of Slavery. (Chicago: The University of Chicago Press, 1970).

Marx, Karl and Engels, Friedrich. On Religion. (New York: Schocken Books, 1964).

Mays, Benjamin Elijah. The Negro's God as Reflected in His Literature. {New York: Russell and Russell, 1968).

Mays, Henry F. The End of American Innocence. (New York: Alfred A. Knopf, 1959).

Meier, August and Rudwick, Elliot. The Making of Black America. (New York: Antheneum Press, 1969).

Myrdal, Gunnar. An American Dilemma: The Negro Problem and Modern Democracy, vol.2. (New York: Harper & Row, 1962), pp. 75, 385-386, 879, 1020.

Mellon, Janes. Bullwhip Days. (New York: Weidenfold Nicholoon, 1988).

Nichols, Charles H. Many Thousands Gone. (Don Mills, Ontario: Fizhenry & Whiteside, Limited, 1969).

Niebuhr, Reinhold. Moral man and Immoral Society. (New York: Charles Scribner's Sons, 1960), pp. 12, 76-77.

Olmstead, Frederick Law. A Journey in the Back Country. (New York: 1860).

Owens, Leslie Howard. This Species of Property. (New York: Oxford University Press, 1976).

Paul, Nathaniel. An Address Delivered on the Celebration of the Abolition of Slavery in the State of New York. (Albany, New York: John B. Van Steenbergh, 1827).

Raboteau, Albert J. Slave Religion. (New York: Oxford University Press, 1978), p. 215.

Rawick, ed. The American Slave: A Composite Antobiography. (Westport, Conn.: Greenwood Press, 1979). Vol. 5, Texas Narratives, pt. 4).

Rice, Duncan C. The Rise and Fall of Black Slavery. (New York: Harper & Row, 1975).

Sellers, James B. Slavery in Alabama. (Tuscaloosa, Alabama: The University of Alabama Press, 1950).

Stampp, Kenneth M. The Peculiar Institution. (New York: Alfred Knopf, 1969), pp. 15-17

Stuckey, Sterling. The Ideological Origins of Black Nationalism. (Boston: BeaconPress, 1972).

"The First Voyage of Robert Baker to Guinie ... 1562," in Richard Hakluyt, The Principal Navigations. Voyages and Discoveries of the English Nation. (London, 1589).

Walker, David, and Garnet, Henry Highland. Walker's Appeal/ Garnet's Address. (Near York: Arno Press, 1969).

Webber, Thomas L. Deep Like the Rivers. (New York: Morton and Company, 1978).

Wilmore, Gayraud S. Black Religion and Black Radicalism. (Garden City, New York: Doubleday & Company, 1972), p. 2.

Woodson, Carter G. <u>The Negro in our History</u>. (Washington, DC: The Associated Publishing, Inc., 1922).

_____. "A Letter of Anthony Burns to the Baptist Church at Union, Fauquier County, Virginia," in <u>The Mind of the Negro as Reflected in Letters Written During The Crisis</u>). (New York: Russell and Russell, 1969).

_____. <u>Negro Orators and Their Orations</u>. (Washington, DC: Associated Publishers, 1925).

Young, Henry James. <u>Major Black Religious Leaders: 1755-1940</u>. (Nashville, Tennessee: Abingdon Press, 1977). pp. 41-42

ABOUT THE AUTHOR

A provocative writer who has done an in-depth study of the subject that will insight further reading. He has taken seriously the task which reveals scholarly research and skillful writing.

www.ingramcontent.com/pod-product-compliance
Lightning Source LLC
Chambersburg PA
CBHW030150100526
44592CB00009B/206